W9-CRN-800

# The
# Backyard Vintner

# The
# Backyard Vintner

## AN ENTHUSIAST'S GUIDE TO GROWING GRAPES AND MAKING WINE AT HOME

Jim Law

CRESTLINE

This edition published in 2011 by CRESTLINE
A division of Book Sales, Inc.
276 Fifth Avenue Suite 206
New York, New York 10001
USA

This edition published by arrangement with Quarry Books, a member
of the Quayside Publishing Group.

First published in the United States of America by
Quarry Books, a member of
Quayside Publishing Group
100 Cummings Center,
Suite 406-L
Beverly, MA 01915-6101
www.rockpub.com

Library of Congress Cataloging-in-Publication Data available

ISBN-13: 978-0-7858-2826-6

10 9 8 7 6 5 4 3 2

Design: Carol Petro
Layout: Susan Fazekas
Cover Image: Cover images:
    Courtesy of Robert Zerkowitz, Wine Institute/
    www.wineinstitute.org,
    (main image); © Marc Grimberg/Alamy, (top, left);
    Clive and Sue Taylor, (middle, left); Guillaume DeLaubier,
    (bottom, left)
Back cover: Fred Stocker
Editor: Pat Price
Illustrations: Michael Yatcko

Printed in China
Reprinted in 2012

# Contents

# Introduction

*T*his book isn't
just about how to
*make* wine, it's about
how to *grow* wine.

*S*o much about wine is wonderful. I'm at peace tending my vines early in the morning, before the rest of the world begins to stir. During the afternoon, simple tasks in the cellar allow me to check on last year's vintage as it evolves and begins to show its character. In the evening, I enjoy the fruits of my labor from many years ago with dinner, making a mental note of that particular growing season as I taste it in the glass. This is why I, like many other winemakers, am so in love with making wine.

This is a practical, simple book for those who love wine and are intrigued with all its aspects: growing, making, and appreciating. Its nuts-and-bolts approach does have one twist, however: It encourages you to base your winemaking decisions not on analysis and lab tests but on taste and intuition. This is how most of the great wines of the world are made.

The winemaking philosophy of this book is traditional, Old World, and noninterventionist. This means that, as much as possible, the wine makes itself, with minimal input by the winemaker. I often find that the more time I spend in the vineyard and the less time I spend in the cellar, the better the wine. I was advised years ago by a French winemaker to "trust your wine." It took me many years to understand that he was telling me to stop trying to tweak the wines by making additions and manipulations and to simply let the wine be itself. I learned—as you can—how to make wines with character and personality rather than seamless, boring perfection.

In many ways, making wine the Old World way is like great cooking: It's intuitive and "hands-on." Learning to make great wine is similar to learning to cook well. As a beginner, you follow recipes carefully, but with time, you learn to cook more intuitively. You taste the soup on the stovetop and know how much salt or vinegar or seasoning to add. If you don't have all the ingredients, you make thoughtful, creative substitutions. This same comfort level can also be reached by the vintner when tasting grapes or fermenting wine and deciding what to do next.

## Terroir

This book isn't just about how to *make* wine; it's about how to *grow* wine. What does this mean? If you envision a vineyard replete with bottles of wine hanging from the vines, you are not far wrong. In fact, the foundation of wine is the vineyard. The true character of a good wine comes from what the French refer to as *terroir*—the taste of the place in which the grapes are grown. A Napa Valley Chardonnay and a French Chablis are made from the same grape variety, yet the wines have nothing in common. Why? The weather and soils in each place are completely different, resulting in wines that, though made from the same grape, do not have the same taste. Discovering the *terroir* from my little patch of earth is the most intellectually stimulating part of the wine growing process.

Warren Winarski, the founder of Stag's Leap Wine Cellar, refers to the "Three G's" that influence your wine: the grape, the ground, and the guy or gal. The grape is important. Chardonnay grapes taste different from Riesling grapes, and each grape variety has its own climate preferences. The ground is much more important. Every slope, change in soil, and minute microclimate difference imparts distinct flavors, aromas, and nuances to a wine. The third G is you. In the wine growing process, you will be putting together a 1,000-piece jigsaw puzzle. The pieces will constantly change as you learn the character of the soils, a vine's vigor, the influences of the weather, and—eventually—the taste of your site.

## Making the Commitment

Is wine growing for you? This book is designed for those who have discovered wine and are inspired to give it a go themselves. But the process of growing grapes and making wine can be very involved.

Your vineyard will be your biggest commitment. Before you head out to the nearest home-renovation store for posts and wire, ask yourself some questions. The most important is do you enjoy gardening? If you do, but have had little or no experience with growing things, I suggest starting a vegetable garden. It is a great way to learn about the seasons, weeds, pests, varieties, soils, and all the fundamentals that go into growing great-tasting food. You will eventually find that wine growing

Your vineyard can take many shapes, from a few rows planted in the yard to hundreds of plants over several acres.

has many similarities. Making the connection from your gardening (or vine-care) decisions and techniques to the quality of the harvest is an important epiphany that all good wine growers must experience.

How much space do you have? You might assume you need acres and acres of property to grow grapes, but you can learn as much with twelve vines as with several hundred. One vine can yield the equivalent of two to five bottles of wine, and two 50-foot (15-meter) rows of vines can produce fifty bottles or more.

How much will it cost? Your largest up-front expense will be establishing the vineyard: Vines, posts, wire, and trellis hardware can take a big bite out of your pocketbook. But once the vineyard is on its way, the financial pressure eases up.

How much patience do you have? It takes years (three or four, to be exact) for your vines to begin producing grapes. This is why you need to be fully enamored with the growing process as well as the final product. Fortunately, winemaking is not as demanding, in terms of time (except at harvest in the early fall); for most of the year, the wine ages quietly without the need for attention from you.

Winemaking requires little space and equipment. In fact, some of the best wines I have ever tasted came from bare-bones cellars with almost primitive equipment. The premise of this book is that you put your heart and soul into the growing of the grapes and then keep the winemaking simple and straightforward. You can get started with winemaking in your kitchen, garage, or cellar with little more than some large buckets, big bottles called carboys, and a siphon tube. As with any avocation, if you find that you want to fine-tune techniques or increase production, there are many opportunities to spend money on equipment. What is much more important is using what you learn from tasting and evaluating your grapes and young wines to make your winemaking decisions. My most important winemaking tool is a wineglass that I keep hanging in my cellar.

This book will help you understand what the winemaking goal is and how to achieve it. It will help you learn to taste critically and develop your palate, so that you can apply your new knowledge throughout the winemaking process. With the globalization of wine, we can have fun exploring good Rieslings from Australia, Sauvignon Blancs from New Zealand, Syrahs from South Africa, or Pinot Noirs from Oregon. But there is nothing more satisfying than tasting a wine from grapevines that you planted in your own backyard.

# The Vineyard

The vineyard is my focus. Soil, site, and microclimate are more important to a great wine than grape variety. I encourage others to strive to be "wine growers."

# Starting
# Your Vineyard

## CHAPTER ONE

*A*rguably, grapevines are the most scrutinized (legal) crop grown in the world. Every detail in their growing, from soil influences and training systems to the timing of harvest, is debated. Wine growers can be particularly opinionated about the superiority of their own techniques, especially after a few glasses of wine.

Each decision you make in the vineyard affects wine flavor, aroma, structure, style, and quality. And even the best growing plan and strategy can be changed by the weather. All of these challenges are what draw people to growing grapes. There is no one best technique, grape variety, soil type, or wine. It is all subjective. In this regard, I consider wine growing to be more art than science.

Many of the most important vineyard decisions are made during the establishment phase. Decisions about vine spacing, variety, and siting become easier once you have experience with your own site. For advice, consult growers in your area. Local vintners with practical experience and a wealth of knowledge have already done some of the trial and error in your locale. Seek them out — there is no substitute for local knowledge.

*A*ny region in which vines are grown provides an opportunity to meet vintners with practical experience and a wealth of knowledge. Seek them out — there is no substitute for local knowledge.

# The Location

Grapevines are extremely adaptable. Over the past few decades, I have seen successful vineyards established in some nontraditional areas. From Quebec to Mexico, and Wales to India, most climatic extremes now host vineyards. In each situation, growers have had to adapt variety selection and growing techniques to their own special piece of earth. Let's look at some of the most important factors you will need to understand before choosing where to plant your vines and which vines to plant.

## ●● Soil

Your site dictates many of your decisions. Understanding your soil characteristics is important. Vines can do well in all kinds of soils, but many grapevine varieties have distinct preferences for certain types of soil. The most important soil characteristic, one that all the world's greatest vineyards share, is excellent drainage. Grapevines do not like "wet feet," meaning they perform poorly, produce substandard grapes, or, in some cases, die if they're planted in soils that stay wet constantly.

How do you know if your soil drains well? Observation helps. It is not a good sign if you notice standing water after rainfall. Slopes tend to have better drainage than flat areas, which is why most, though not all, vineyards are located on hillsides. You can also visit your local farm extension office for a map of the soil in your area. If you find your site on a soil map, you can determine the soil type and its drainage characteristics. Because drainage is so important to so many aspects of farming and building, soil-type drainage characteristics are usually well documented.

Soil fertility is another consideration. Vines do not produce high-quality grapes in rich, vigorous, highly organic soils, which is counterintuitive to most gardeners. The well-worked, fertile soils that are ideal for vegetables and flower gardens can be disastrous for grapevines. Vines supplied with abundant nutrients and water can go "vegetative," meaning they want to grow only leaves at the expense of producing and ripening fruit. Vines need to slow down and stop producing new leaves in the late summer so that they can concentrate their energy on ripening the grapes.

Throughout this section, I often refer to a "balanced" vine. This is a vine that naturally grows just the right amount of leaves to fully ripen its fruit. If the soil is too rich, the vine will overproduce leaves. Excessive leaf

*tip*

One of the wonderful mysteries of growing wine grapes is trying to understand the concept of *terroir*, the aromas and flavors that a vineyard site gives to the wine. Your site will have its own *terroir*, but you cannot know what those flavors will be until you start making wine from your own grapes.

Slopes provide good soil drainage, air flow, and sun exposure. Usually the steeper the slope, the higher the grape quality. The vines in this newly planted vineyard sport grow tubes.

*tip*

Vines like lots of sun. Do not plant them close to trees or buildings that block the southern sun (or northern sun in the Southern Hemisphere).

shading produces fewer and lesser-quality grapes. It is relatively easy to add nutrients or organic matter if a vine is too weak but literally impossible to remove them from soil that contains too much.

### Slope

Vines like a good, steep slope. Steep hillsides are usually well drained and, because of years of erosion, are typically low in nutrients and organic matter. However, grapegrowers don't always plant on steep slopes because of the difficulty in tending the vines. Hills can be physically exhausting, awkward to work, and dangerous if one uses power equipment.

### Aspect

Aspect refers to the direction in which the slope faces. In the cooler regions of the Northern Hemisphere, southern slopes are desirable to maximize heat and sun. However, a southern slope may not be desirable if you are in a warm growing region or are interested in growing white wine grapes that need cooler ripening conditions.

### Accessibility

Out of sight, out of mind—locate your vineyard close to home. During the growing season, you will need to tend your vines regularly. At harvest time, you will be checking the grapes for flavors and predators almost daily. Tools and water also need to be accessible.

## The Weather

In general, grapevines can grow in all types of weather. What variety you choose to plant will depend greatly on the climate conditions in your area. Huge differences in variety adaptability exist, as we will see on pages 24 and 25 . It's important that you understand the climate constraints for your area. There is no one region in which all varieties can flourish.

Length of growing season refers to the average number of frost-free days during the growing season. This information is important because some grape varieties need a long growing season for the grapes to ripen.

### Frost

Frost is defined as the temperature that kills green tissue on vines. Wind and humidity can influence the temperature at which a killing frost will occur. Usually a temperature of 28°F (–2°C) will damage or kill most green tissue on a vine. Dormant buds, canes, and trunks will be fine.

Most of our concern is with a late spring frost. By this time, the vines have already budded out (you can see green leaves forming). If the temperature falls below 28°F (–2°C), these new succulent shoots will be killed. Unfortunately for the grower, these shoots carry most of that season's crop. Although the vine will produce secondary shoots, depending on the variety, they will produce few clusters of grapes.

A concern at the other end of the growing season is an early fall frost, which can freeze the leaves needed to ripen any grapes still on the vines. Once frosted, these leaves will fall off the vine. If this happens, the season has, for all practical purposes, come to an end, regardless of whether the grapes are ripe.

The vines need these leaves not only to ripen a crop but also to prepare for the winter. Leaves are needed late in the season to ripen the vines' wood and to store carbohydrates for the winter and following spring. If the season is cut short by frost, the vines are weakened. In regions with cold winters, this situation could lead to significant winter-related dieback.

Topography plays a role in where frost occurs, which can be very localized. Most frosts occur late at night under still, cloudless conditions. Cold air, which is heavier than warm air, flows to the lowest areas, which are appropriately called frost pockets. Above the cold air is the relatively warm air, which forms what is called the thermal zone. This zone is where you want your vineyard to be. Observation, local knowledge, and strategically placed thermometers will help you determine the location of your area's frost pockets.

Large bodies of water can affect frost damage, as well. Water retains heat or cold temperatures longer than land does. In the spring, areas close to water are cooler; therefore, the growing season will begin later than it will further inland. With luck, this delay can postpone bud break long enough to avoid a late spring frost. In the fall, the body of water keeps the nearby land warmer, which can extend the growing season.

These bodies of water need to be quite large. Oceans qualify, as do very large lakes such as the Great Lakes or New York's Finger Lakes. Farm ponds and streams are too small to have any effect on the growing season.

*tip*

If you are in an area new to grape growing, try to plant as many varieties as possible. This can be logistically difficult during the winemaking stage but is invaluable during the long learning curve in the vineyard

Climate is an important consideration when choosing grape varieties. The afternoon sun on a July day could damage grapes in a hot, dry area, but in cooler climates, the warmth is welcome.

Hilly areas generate what are called thermal air inversions, in which air at the top of a rise is warmer than the air at the bottom, in the "valley." During still nights, the coldest air flows down to the valley floor, forming a frost pocket. The layer of relatively warm air that rises above this cold air is known as the thermal zone. This is where you want to locate your vineyard. Be careful not to situate your vineyard too high in elevation, or you will have moved out of the thermal zone and back into cold air.

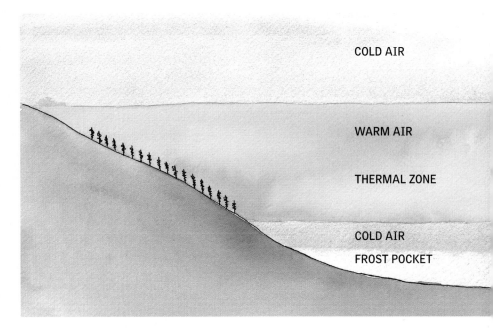

COLD AIR

WARM AIR

THERMAL ZONE

COLD AIR
FROST POCKET

## ●● Freeze

Freeze is defined as temperatures cold enough to damage dormant vines in the winter. If you live in an area in which winter temperatures fall below 0°F (−18°C), this low temperature could be the most important factor in choosing which varieties to plant. Some varieties have been bred specifically for cold hardiness and will survive temperatures colder than −20°F (−29°C), but most varieties would suffer significant damage or death (see the chart on pages 24 and 25).

Freeze damage to grapevines can express itself in three progressively devastating ways. First is bud damage. The fruitful buds in vines are usually damaged beginning at temperatures below −5°F (−20°C). Trunks can be damaged at temperatures below −10°F (−23°C), and vine death can occur at temperatures below −15°F (−26°C). Much of this damage depends on the vine variety. In a few very cold regions, wine growers bury their vines in the fall by removing them from the trellis wires, laying them on the ground, and covering them with soil. The soil is an insulator and protects the vines from damaging cold temperatures.

## ●● Heat

At the other end of the spectrum is excessive heat. If temperatures exceed 95°F (35°C) during the growing season, the vines essentially shut down to conserve water. High temperatures during ripening time can interfere with ripening and hurt quality. The heat causes white grapes to lose too much acidity and red grapes to lose color and tannins. Ideally, grapes should ripen when the nights are cool (below 60°F [15°C]) and the days warm (in the 70s°F [21° to 26°C]). This is why later-ripening varieties typically produce the best quality wine in hot growing areas. They ripen when the weather moderates in the fall.

## ●● Rainfall

Vines can handle a fairly wide range of rainfall, from a little to a lot. More important than *how much* rain falls is *when* the rain falls. Winter and spring are good times for abundant rain to replenish soil moisture. During the summer, vines prefer relatively dry conditions, with the occasional replenishing rain or irrigation. In the fall, most growers prefer to see little or no rain, for three reasons. First, if rain soaks the soil, the vines' roots take up this water and transfer it to the grapes. The water dilutes the flavors, sugars, and acidity of the grape juice and, in turn, the resulting wine. Second, prolonged rain can bring rot. Rotten grapes make awful wine and must be discarded. Third, if it is raining, the sun is not shining. The sun is what makes fine wine—little sun, little photosynthesis.

## The Grapes

Finding the grape varieties that do well on your site can take years of trial and error. Fortunately, much of that work has probably already been done in your region. Because grapes are now grown in most areas of the world, some local knowledge can be found just about everywhere. Hundreds of grape varieties are

## *Cabernet Sauvignon*

Cabernet Sauvignon grapes produce distinctive, tannic wines that are long-aging (five to ten years for peak flavor) and often blended with other wines to give them more complexity. Barrel-aging for as long as eighteen months before bottling is common. The primary grape variety grown in the Medoc region of Bordeaux, Cabernet Sauvignon requires warm growing conditions to reach maturity.

**Taste Characteristics:** cedar, tobacco, dark cherry, black currant, sometimes green pepper or olive when grown in cool climates.
**Serve:** at 60°F (15°C) to 65°F (18°C)
**Pair with:** Grilled red meats.

Something to keep in mind when determining where to locate your vineyard is accessibility. This vineyard (above) is conveniently located near the house. It has the further advantage of being on a slope, a plus when it comes to drainage.

available to choose from. This section will help you understand the parameters, categories, and characteristics that could be important for your situation. If you are in love with a certain wine, I urge you to try that grape variety, at least experimentally. Because home winemakers often make wines in 5-gallon (19-liter) batches, I recommend planting at least ten vines per variety, depending on the vine spacing you choose to use (see page 28). Vines are not cross-pollinated, so you can plant a single variety, but I recommend trying several.

## ●● The Three Parameters

In Europe, most regions are planted with the grape varieties that consistently produce good wine. We won't talk about how many hundreds of years of trial and error this feat required. Those who are new to grape-growing and who live in nontraditional viticultural areas need to eliminate varieties that may have serious difficulties adapting to the site. Three questions that must be asked when choosing a variety are: will it survive; will it consistently produce a crop; and will it make wine that you like to drink?

**Survivability**   Extremely cold winter temperatures, diseases, and insects can eliminate the choice of many varieties in certain regions. If temperatures in your area fall below 0°F (–18°C), you will need to research the cold hardiness of the variety you choose. Diseases such as Pierce's disease in California and the southern United States and grapevine yellows in Europe, Australia, and the eastern United States can slowly kill some varieties, whereas others are less affected. The infamous insect phylloxera (see phylloxera, page 67), will damage the roots of some varieties but not others.

**Consistent Production**   Weather, specifically rain, can keep some varieties from producing consistently from one year to the next. Some varieties have difficulty with pollination in cool, cloudy, or rainy conditions. This limitation leads to poor fruit set (also known as *coulure*) and a meager crop. Bunch rot is an issue in regions experiencing rain near harvest time. With certain thin-skinned varieties, a beautiful crop can turn to mush in a matter of days if rain arrives at the wrong time.

**Wine Quality**   If your area is limited in suitable varieties with which you are unfamiliar, you should taste wines made from the grapes you are considering. This is primarily true in regions where cold winter temperatures severely limit the possible varieties you can grow successfully.

If you plan to grow grapes in a region with little wine growing experience, consider yourself a pioneer, and go into it with the attitude that it will take many years to sort it out. Getting there is the fun part (provided you have patience, enthusiasm, and a fairly stable bank account).

## ●● Grape Categories

There are three general classifications of grape varieties, loosely grouped by species. All of the following are of the genus Vitis.

- *Vitis vinifera*   *Vinifera,* the Old World/European grapes, are the most widely grown and most commonly known. The varieties include most of the wines you would see in any wine shop: Cabernet Sauvignon, Merlot, Syrah, Chardonnay, and Riesling. These grapes are considered to have the highest potential to make great wine. Naturally, they can be the most difficult to grow and are the most susceptible to problems with disease and cold temperatures.

- **French-American hybrids**   These grapes are crosses of the more resilient Native American grapes with the tender *Vitis vinifera.* They are also referred to as interspecific hybrids, because they are crosses of several varieties. Most were developed in the late 1800s by a massive French breeding program to find vines that both were resistant to phylloxera and mildews and produced good wine. Because the program was a government project, these varieties were given numbers instead of names. They have since been named but are often still referred to by number.

French-American hybrids are adaptable to widely different climate situations and disease pressures. Most are resistant to phylloxera damage, but more and more commercial producers are grafting them to commonly available rootstocks anyway because the hybrids respond better to grafting. Commonly grown varieties include Seyval, Vidal, Foch, and Chambourcin.

## *Clones*

When you order *vinifera* vines from the nursery, you will probably be asked which clone you would like. *Vinifera* vines have been cultivated for many centuries. Over the years, slight differences in individual vines have been observed. Cuttings were taken from these vines and propagated for certain special qualities: one vine produced grapes that were smaller; another was more aromatic; and another earlier ripening.

In the old days, these clones were given names, such as Pommard or Martini. More recently, universities have implemented a more scientific approach to clonal selections, meticulously growing and evaluating them in test plots and releasing to the public the best performers, which are often labeled with a number.

Clonal characteristics can be minor, and most commercial growers will plant several different clones of one variety, for no other reason than to achieve greater complexity of flavor in the wine. Clonal selection is still a relatively new phenomenon in most of the world. Because most growers have little experience with different clones, we are really only guessing which ones will do best on a given site.

● **Native American .** This broad category of different species and crosses originates from native wild American vines. Most are "chance hybrids" (seeds from European vines randomly cross-pollinated by wild vines) discovered centuries ago by early American settlers. Some are more recent, intentional hybrids. Native American vines tend to be the most cold hardy and disease-resistant and are well suited for novice backyard growers in less than ideal climates. The wines produced from these varieties, however, can be very assertive and distinct. Varieties include Delaware, Catawba, Norton, and Frontenac.

## *Grafting*

To graft a vine, a piece of dormant budwood from the fruitful variety (the scion), for example Pinot Noir, is matched to a stick of rootstock. The two pieces are fit together and then quickly dipped in melted grafting wax. The wax hardens and protects the graft union from drying out.

The newly grafted vines are then placed temporarily in a greenhouse, until the graft union joins—or calluses over—and the roots grow. After a few months, the tender vines are transplanted to the field, where they grow out for the rest of the season. In the fall, they are dug up; sorted according to rooting, scion growth, and graft union quality; and shipped in the early spring.

●● **Rootstocks**

In most grapegrowing areas, *vinifera*, and some French-American hybrids, are grafted onto rootstocks. The principle reason for grafting is for resistance to phylloxera. Rootstocks can also help a vine adapt to unusual soil conditions, such as high pH or excessive iron content. In some cases, rootstocks can have a slight impact on vine vigor. Most rootstocks were hybridized by French and German researchers after the phylloxera devastation. The researchers crossed different species of mostly native American vines to obtain rooting characteristics that worked well for specific soil conditions. Resistance to phylloxera was paramount, but roots that could grow well in calcareous or high-iron soils were also important for specific regions.

# Climate and Variety Characteristics for Grape

| | Climate Characteristics | Vine Characteristics | Possible Varieties |
|---|---|---|---|
| *Hot and Dry* | Hot, sunny days, cooler nights. Unlimited growing season, in terms of ripening. Irrigation usually required. | Any grape variety can grow and produce grapes in this climate. However, wine from grapes that ripen under hot conditions usually lack character and structure. Very late-ripening varieties are your best bet. | **REDS** *Grenache* Very vigorous and disease susceptible. Wine quality is yield dependent. Also makes wonderful rosés.<br><br>*Mourvèdre* Buds late and ripens late. Needs a long growing season. Very soil adaptable in hot climates. From Spain, but widely grown in southern France. |
| *Hot and Humid* | Hot, humid days, with rain and cloud cover possible throughout the growing season. Warm, dewy nights. Unlimited growing season, in terms of ripening. | Diseases, especially bunch rots, are a concern. Varieties that ripen late in the season (when nights are cool) and produce loose clusters and grapes with thicker, rot-resistant skins are ideal. | **REDS** *Tannat* Late budding, disease-resistant, productive. Makes a dark-colored, rustic, long-lived wine. From the Madiran region of southwest France. |
| *Temperate and Dry* | Warm to hot, sunny days and cool nights. Some late-season varieties in some vintages may not ripen in this climate. Late spring frosts can be a problem. Irrigation may be helpful. | A wide range of major grape varieties do well in this climate. Avoid very early- or very late-ripening varieties. | **REDS** *Syrah* Late budding, ripens midseason. High vigor. Some rot and berry shriveling problems. Classic grape of northern Rhône; known as *Shiraz* in Australia. |
| *Temperate and Humid* | Warm to hot days and warm nights in midsummer. Regular rainfall and morning dews throughout growing season, including harvest. Growing season too short to ripen late-season varieties. | Many varieties can do well, but rain, especially at harvest, cause rot and quality problems. Varieties that ripen in midseason and are resistant to bunch rots are your best bets. | **REDS** *Merlot* Low-vigor vine produces large berries. Fruit set can be a problem if there is rain during bloom, midseason ripening.<br><br>*Cabernet Franc* Prolific vine, high-vigor, mid-late season ripening. Needs well-drained soils. Wines distinctly herbal. |
| *Cool and Dry* | Warm days and cool nights. Short growing season and low temperatures can limit ripening, except in microclimates that have great sun exposure and ocean or large lake influences. Limited rainfall and low humidity during the growing season. | Early-ripening varieties. | **REDS** *Pinot Noir* Classic red grape of Burgundy. Does well in only a few special cool microclimates. Thin skins susceptible to rot. A very difficult grape to grow and wine to make.<br><br>*Gamay* Vigorous, rot-susceptible, early-ripening, productive grape from Beaujolais. |
| *Cool and Humid* | Warm days and cool, dewy nights. Summertime and fall rains. Short growing season. | Early ripening, rot resistant. Cold hardiness may be required for regions experiencing winter temperatures below −5°F (−20°C). | **REDS** *Foch* Small clusters, disease-resistant, early-ripening, cold-hardy vine. Produces dark-colored, early-drinking, distinctively flavored wine. |
| *Limiting Cold* | Defined by cold winter temperatures, regularly falling below −15°F (−26°C). Growing season short and cool. | Cold hardiness and early ripening are the most important attributes. All varieties listed are Minnesota and Swenson hybrids. | **REDS** *St. Croix* Vigorous and hardy, moderate acidity and sugar. Widely grown in Quebec, New England, and the upper midwestern United States. |

# Growing

It can be difficult to decide what grape varieties to plant, especially in non-traditional grape rowing regions, and there are hundreds, if not thousands, of grape varieties from which to choose. This simple chart applies some general attributes to commonly grown varieties. Note that these are very general guidelines, and in each category you will almost certainly find exceptions to the rule. Local growers are your best source of information.

## Possible Varieties (continued)

*Sangiovese* Thin skins and rot-susceptible. Large clusters mean it can easily overcrop. Many different clones.

*Cabernet Sauvignon* Vigorous vine. Needs well-drained, low-fertility soils. Late ripening, thick skins. Wines have great tannins and depth.

**WHITES** *Marsanne* Vigorous, high-yielding vine. Makes a full-bodied, low-acid, short-lived wine. From the Rhône Valley.

*Malvasia* Vigorous, productive vine. Likes dry climates and well-drained soils. Wines are full-bodied and very aromatic. Many different varieties and clones of Malvasia exist, including red versions, mostly from Italy.

*Petit Verdot* Bordeaux variety. Small black berries, late-ripening. High acid and high sugar. Dark-colored, rustic wine.

*Norton* (*Cynthiana*) Small grapes and clusters, disease-resistant, late-ripening, small crops. Dense, high-acid wine. Originates from Virginia.

**WHITES** *Vidal* Thick skins, rot-resistant, late ripening. Potentially large crops. Known especially for dessert-style, but also makes good dry wine.

*Petit Manseng* Small berries and clusters. Very late-ripening, with high acidity. Best known for the dessert wines of Jurançon in southwest France.

*Zinfandel* Adaptable to many dry climates, especially in California. Uneven ripening and rot can be a problem.

*Tempranillo* From Rioja, Spain. Early-ripening, vigorous, makes a low-acid, highly structured wine.

**WHITES** *Chardonnay* Very adaptable to many climates, mid-season ripening. Early-budding and frost susceptible. Powdery mildew can be a problem. Classic grape for white Burgundies.

*Sauvignon Blanc* Tight clusters, thin-skinned. Very vigorous. Early-ripening.

*Chenin Blanc* High-vigor vines are rot-susceptible. Can make intense dry or sweet wines in Loire, but has been abused in the New World by overcropping and planting in hot regions, making bland, neutral wines.

*Chambourcin* Early budding, low-vigor, late ripening, disease-resistant. Makes an herbal, high-acid, low-tannin wine that blends well with higher tannin varieties.

**WHITES** *Viognier* Fairly rot-resistant, mid-season ripening. Can have some set problems. Makes perfumed, full-bodied wines when ripe.

*Vidal* Late ripening, thick skinned, large clusters, rot resistant. Best known for making sweet, late-harvest wines, but also can make good dry wines.

*Traminette* A recent hybrid with 50 percent Gewürztraminer. Has good disease-resistance and cold-hardiness. Similar flavor profile to Gewürztraminer.

**WHITES** *Riesling* Relatively late ripening. Has sour rot problems if it ripens in warm, humid conditions. Can make good, light, aromatic wines at low ripeness levels or intense, sweet wines at high ripeness, especially when infected by botrytis rot.

*Gewürztraminer* Very early ripening and very rot-susceptible. Pink berries on tight, compact clusters. Makes high-alcohol, low-acid wines with distinct spicy aromas.

*Pinot Gris* Also known as *Pinot Grigio* in Italy and *Ruländer* in Germany. When ripe, clusters are pink. If vines produce moderate to low yields and grapes are picked ripe, wines have intense perfume, low acidity, and great body. If overcropped and picked early, wines are light and tart.

*Landot Noir* Late bud break, early ripening, disease resistant, cold hardy, very vigorous.

**WHITES** *Delaware* Small clusters with pink berries. Cold hardy, early ripening, high Brix. Distinctly aromatic wines. Originates from Delaware, Ohio.

*Seyval* Very productive, low-vigor, cold-hardy vines can be severly overcropped, resulting in early decline. Somewhat bunch rot-susceptible in warmer regions. Also known as *Seyve-Villard 5276*.

*Frontenac* Very vigorous and productive. Disease resistant, very cold hardy. High sugar and high acid.

**WHITES** *Louise Swenson* Very cold hardy and disease-resistant. Easy vine to grow in northern climates. Late bud break.

*La Crescent* Somewhat susceptible to powdery and downy mildew. Makes very aromatic wines with character. A new selection from the University of Minnesota.

*Prairie Star* Very cold hardy but some disease susceptibility. Fruit set and shoot breakage from wind can be a problem. Wines have more body than many northern varieties, making it a good blender.

# Planting

## CHAPTER TWO

*A*lthough planting the vines does not take long and is fairly straightforward, the preplanting decisions you need to make can be somewhat complex and daunting. How big should your vineyard be? What about vine spacing? How do you orient the rows? Should you add anything to the soil?

Ideally, you should address these questions the year before planting, to give you enough time to order vines and incorporate any soil amendments. Every region has its own soil requirements, and unless you happen to have a degree in agronomy or soil science, you will need to get a professional evaluation and recommendations for your soil conditions. Fortunately, most regions of the world have an extensive agriculture support system in place that can help you with this.

*P*lanting a new vineyard is a rewarding job that fills you with a sense of adventure and great expectation of discovery. You are working with soil that will eventually express itself in your wine.

## Soil Preparation

Before you plant, you must perform several steps and make some decisions. You need to learn as much as you can about your soil. I have discussed the importance of drainage. You also need to understand your soil's fertility. Send a soil sample to the appropriate local government or co-op farm advisor for analysis. Knowing your soil's pH, nutrient levels, and organic matter content will enable you to amend your soil well in advance of planting.

● **pH** Vines can grow in a wide range of soil pH, but a level between 6.0 and 6.5 is considered ideal for nutrient uptake. If your soil is acidic (lower than 6.0), you should incorporate lime into your soil. If your soil is basic (a pH level higher than 7.0), you may need to find varieties or rootstocks that are adapted to limestone (higher pH) soils. For both lime and nutrient additions, follow the recommendations of your local farm advisor. Every area has unique soil circumstances.

● **Nutrients** Vines are not demanding when it comes to nutrients. They are light feeders and fairly adaptable. In a few cases, fertilization may be necessary. If your soil test results show nutrient deficiencies, seek professional advice on amending the situation. University courses and books on grapevine nutrition are good sources of information on the topic.

● **Organic matter** The percentage of organic matter in your soil can be a good indicator of the potential vigor of your vines. Soils with more than two percent organic matter may result in some vigorously growing vines, especially in clay soils in combination with lots of summer rainfall.

## Laying Out the Vineyard

When laying out your vineyard, consider the direction, width, and length of your vine rows. To maximize the yield of a typical backyard grower's small parcel of land, rows and vines are often planted closer together than in commercial operations.

*tip*

Adding amendments without knowing what is already in your soil is a mistake. Too much of one nutrient or another can throw the vine off balance. An excessive amount of potassium in the soil, for example, can cause the vine to take in more potassium than it needs, to the exclusion of magnesium, which can lead to a magnesium deficiency. Adding compost and manure may be a good idea if your soil is depleted and low in organic matter but can stimulate excessive growth if the soil is already fertile.

This vineyard might have some shading and disease problems. The tall trees and vigorous, closely spaced vines prevent sunlight penetration and air circulation to dry out the leaves and grapes after a rain or heavy dew. Mildews and rots thrive in moist conditions.

For most backyard grapegrowers, land is a premium; the goal is to maximize its use by planting vines and rows close together. If the vine rows are too close together, however, one row will shade the next when the sun is lower in the sky (mornings, late afternoons, and later in the fall).

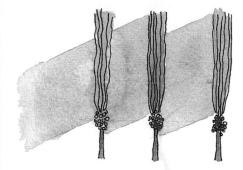

*tip*

A few calculations can help you estimate how much wine your vineyard may ultimately produce. Because of differences in vine spacing and training systems, I prefer to estimate how much wine will be produced from a given trellis row length. One hundred feet (30.5 m) of well-tended vines will produce 8 to 13 gallons (40 to 65 750-ml bottles) of wine. (Each meter [yard] of vine row yields about 1 to 1.5 liters of wine.)

## Row Orientation

For ease of care, the best airflow, and maximum sunlight capture, I recommend planting vines on trellises in rows. Row orientation (the direction your rows take) is often decided by circumstances such as the slope or configuration of your available space. For example, if you have a long, narrow piece of land, it is more practical to plant the rows so that there are a few long rows rather than many short ones. As you will see in the chapter on trellis construction, installing numerous end posts and anchors can be expensive (and time consuming). Although not hugely important, the most efficient row orientation for sun capture is north/south. In very hot, sunny Northern Hemisphere regions, rows are often angled slightly at southwest to northeast to reduce the intensity of the hottest afternoon sun on the west side of the vine leaves.

## Vine Spacing

When deciding how to lay out your rows, you must make two separate decisions: how much distance to leave between rows, and how much distance to leave between vines within the rows.

**Between Rows**   Space your rows so that there is enough room between them to work them comfortably. If they are too close together, it can be difficult to maneuver while working, and one row can shade the next. Spacing rows too far apart is simply a waste of land, which, for the backyard grower, can be valuable. I suggest spacing the rows a minimum of 5' (1.5 meters) apart. Less than 5' between rows can result in one row shading the next and poor air circulation (the canopy needs to dry quickly for disease control). If you plan to use a tractor, riding mower, or any other type of vehicle for maintenance, space the rows at least 2' (61 cm) wider than the width of the vehicle to give you enough maneuverability. If you are tending the vineyard by hand, 5' or 6' (1.5 to 2 meters) between rows will maximize your available space.

**Between Vines**   Spacing between vines can range from less than 3' to more than 8' (.9 to 2.5 meters)—a huge variability (see "Vine Density," page 30. I recommend that you base your vine spacing on potential vine vigor. High soil fertility (deep clay soils with lots of organic matter); a long, hot growing season; and abundant rainfall encourage vigorous vine growth. In these conditions, I recommend spacing the vines further apart (6' [2 m] or more). In poorer soils, especially in dry regions, closer vine spacing may be more appropriate.

Once you have determined your vineyard layout and vine spacing, order your vines as soon as possible. Finding small quantities of specific varieties can be difficult if left to the last minute. I highly recommend ordering vines as much as one year in advance to ensure availability (see Resources, page 167).

## Planting

Once you have made your decisions concerning varieties and spacing, it's time to get down and dirty. This is the beauty of wine growing—it is both intellectual and physical.

### ●● When to Plant

Planting is typically done in the early spring, once the soil has dried adequately; you want it to be loose and friable. I prefer to get an early jump on planting so that the vines can benefit from spring rains and settle in before the growing season starts. It is fine to plant dormant vines before a frost, because frost damages only green growth.

Most vineyardists prefer spring planting, but fall planting is an option for regions in which winters are not cold enough to cause vine damage. Many nurseries, however, will not have vines ready until spring.

### ●● Preparing Your Vines

Most nurseries sell one-year-old, bare-rooted, dormant vines. These vines are cuttings or grafts that the nursery has grown in their fields to establish a root system. After a year, they are dug up, bundled, and shipped bare rooted.

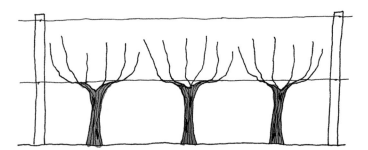

## *Vine Density*

Of all the philosophies and theories in grapegrowing, vine density (spacing between vines) is probably the most controversial and most difficult to understand. The argument for high density (close spacing) is that each individual vine needs to produce only a small amount of grapes. These grapes will have more intense flavor than a larger vine that has to ripen more grapes. Low density (wider spacing) advocates argue that if soil and climate conditions warrant vigorous growth, the vines should be given more room to spread out, making for a more balanced vine—one that naturally produces just the right amount of shoot growth to fill out the trellis space allocated to it.

In many of the great European estates, typical spacings are approximately 39" (1 m) between vines and 39" to 59" (1 to 1.5 m) between rows. Their reasoning is that high-quality wine grapes are produced when each vine has to ripen only a small amount of fruit (six or seven clusters, or just 2 or 3 pounds (1 kg) per vine. Most of these estates are on less fertile, root-restrictive soils.

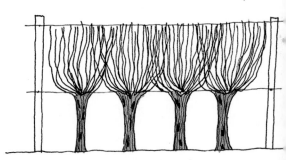

How much space to leave between vines within each row has been an ongoing debate, especially in new viticultural areas. Advocates for close spacing argue that each vine will need to ripen fewer clusters, the result being more concentration and intensity in the wine. Adherents to the theory of wider spacing believe that in deep, rich soils, vines need more room to grow shoots and roots and are more balanced at wider spacings.

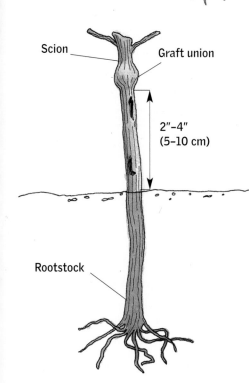

Your vines will usually arrive bare-rooted and in bundles of twenty-five. It is critical to keep the roots moist and cool until planted. This vine was dipped in blue wax by the nursery to protect the graft union from drying out. Once planted, the new shoots will break through the wax.

Scion

Graft union

2"–4"
(5–10 cm)

Rootstock

If your vines are grafted, plant them so that the graft union (the swollen area below the buds) is 2" to 4" (5 to 10 cm) above the ground.

When your vines arrive from the nursery, make sure the roots are moist. If you cannot plant them right away, store in a cool (not freezing) spot, and keep moist by spraying with water and wrapping tightly in the plastic bags in which they were shipped. Avoid immersing the roots in water for longer than twenty-four hours because they can asphyxiate. Do not store vines at a temperature higher than 55°F (13°C) for more than a week or two, or they will start to grow in the box, which can weaken them.

It is not necessary to trim your vines, because the nursery will usually trim them before shipping. You may want to trim the roots, though, to about 8" (20.5 cm), so that they can spread out uniformly in the planting hole. If the vine tops are not trimmed, you may want to trim them down to two to four buds.

## ●● Planting Your Vines

Planting vines is fairly straightforward. Dig a hole wide enough to accommodate the roots when they are spread out. The hole should be deep enough so that, in the case of grafted vines, the graft union (the swollen area just below the top buds) (see illustration at left) is 2" to 4" (5 to 10 cm) above the soil surface to prevent scion rooting. (The scion will root if it is in contact with the soil, negating the reason for grafting onto the rootstock.) Planting depth for nongrafted vines is not as critical, as long as the buds are above ground.

The biggest concern during planting is root damage from the wind and sun. Keep the vines in a bucket of water that you carry from hole to hole. As soon as you position the vine in the hole, cover the roots with soil, and lightly tamp down the loose soil around the roots with your hands.

As long as the soil is damp during planting, it is not necessary to water dormant vines right away. Once they show green shoots and leaves and begin growing, they will need good soil moisture. You will need to water your newly planted vines if you haven't had a few soaking rains.

There is no easy rule of thumb as to how much water is needed—much depends on the soil type. Whereas clay soils retain lots of water, sandy soils need water more frequently. One drenching rain or watering will go a long way. If subsequent conditions are hot and dry, dig down into the soil a few inches. If the soil is dry, water, if possible. If the soil is cool and moist, don't worry. Once planted, with one good watering or rainfall, it would be rare for a vine to die due to lack of water. However, it may not grow much in the first year if conditions are too dry.

# The Trellis

rapevines grow best, when trained to a trellis—the posts, wire, and other hardware support the vine. Vines are still grown without trellises, especially in hot, dry areas where disease pressure from rainfall and humidity is not a concern. However, it is widely agreed that training vines on wires improves vine health and grape quality and makes the vines easier to work. During the growing season, you will need to tend to your vine's canopy—the actively growing parts of the vine, including the shoots, leaves, and grape clusters. Performing this task is easier if the canopy is at a convenient height off the ground.

Vines are susceptible to many diseases that can be persistent under wet or humid conditions. Holding the vine's leaves and fruit off the ground helps dry out the canopy and reduces disease pressure. Vine leaves also need to be well exposed to sunlight for best fruit growth. Trellises allow the leaves to maximize sunlight interception.

*Training vines improves vine health and grape quality and makes the vines easier to work.*

# Basic Trellis Installation

The earlier you put up your trellis, the better. If the first year of vine growth is rapid, you will need to support the tender shoots. Plan to have your trellis up within a few months of planting. If possible, have the posts in the ground before planting—they can help as planting guides, to ensure the vines are planted straight in the rows. Installing posts also requires a lot of working space, which could be compromised by having to step delicately around planted vines.

# Materials

## ●● Posts

Posts hold the wires, which in turn hold the vines. You will use two types of posts: end posts and line posts. End posts are obviously the posts at either end of the rows. They take most of the weight of the vines and need to be especially strong and well anchored. Line posts, which are the posts between the end posts, are generally less sturdy.

Posts are usually made of wood or metal, depending on availability and price. Line posts are usually 8' (2.5 m) tall, so they can be set 2' (61 cm) into the ground and still be 6' (2 m) above ground. End posts are usually set deeper into the ground and angled back for better anchoring. Eight-foot (2.5 m) end posts will work, but the trellis will be shorter at the ends. Ten-foot (3 m) posts, which can be expensive and difficult to find, are ideal.

Posts should be no more than 24' (7.5 m) apart within the row. If you have a strong back, sandy soil, and a small vineyard, it is possible to install the posts by digging the holes with a shovel or manual posthole digger. Otherwise, I recommend renting a gas-powered auger.

## ●● Anchor Systems

Because the end posts take a tremendous amount of strain, they need to be anchored so that they are not pulled inward. To do this, bury an anchor about 3' (1 m) into the ground, about 6' (2 m) away from the base of the post, with a brace wire attached to both it and the end post. I have seen many ingenious objects used as anchors, ranging from cinder blocks to old tires, but the most common are helix/screw earth anchors.

Helix anchors are widely available. In nonrocky soils, they can be screwed into the ground by turning a crowbar or digging bar inserted in the anchor's eye. Short rows (less than 100' (30.5 m) can get by with smaller anchors (2' [61 cm] long). Longer rows need more anchoring, so go with the longest and widest anchors available.

# Installing the Trellis

This is an example of a basic trellis system for simple Guyot (vertical shoot positioned) training. You can modify it to suit the availability of materials and to different vine-training systems.

a) Line posts are usually 8' (2.5 m) long and can be made from wood or metal. They are typically set 2' (61 cm) into the ground, leaving 6' (2 m) above ground. Set them no more than 24' (7.5 m) apart.

b) End posts take most of the weight and strain of the trellis load and need to be stronger than line posts. They are often angled back to better withstand the pull of the wires. Ideally, they are set 3' (90 cm) into the ground, with 7' (2.1 m) protruding aboveground at an angle. These posts are very expensive. You can substitute shorter end posts—just be sure that the first line post is within 12' (4 m) of the end post so that the trellis is tall enough.

c) Anchors keep the end posts from being pulled into the trellis by the wires. A screw anchor is shown here, but many other materials can be used. Try to bury your anchors 2' to 3' (61 to 90 cm) into the ground.

d) Attach a looped brace wire from the anchor to the top of the end post, and tighten it by inserting a twitch stick

(e) between the looped wires and turning it until the brace wire becomes taut.

f) Trellis wires are most commonly 12.5-gauge, high-tensile wires. Avoid using plastic or smaller-gauge wire that could be cut by pruning shears, or you will be spending a lot of time splicing after pruning season.

g) The wires are looped around the end post and then attached back to themselves using a crimping sleeve (see illustration on page 37). They can also be wrapped around the end post several times and then secured by a trellis staple (see illustration[directional]) that is pounded all the way in, until flush with the wood.

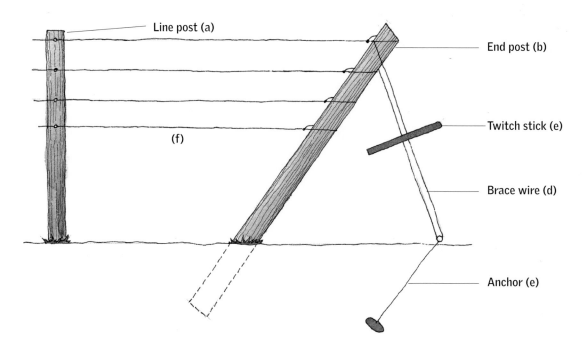

Line post (a)

(f)

End post (b)

Twitch stick (e)

Brace wire (d)

Anchor (e)

Make sure to use brace wire, not trellis wire, to attach the end post to the anchor. Brace wire is made to withstand this tensioning, whereas trellis wire is not. Make a loop from the anchor to the end post and back again, and then tighten the wire using a "twitch stick," a stick turned in the loop to twist the two strands of brace wire.

## Wires

Use 12.5-gauge, high-tensile fencing wire for trellis wire. As with most of the materials you use for your trellis, this wire is available at farm-supply stores, co-ops, or from specialty catalogs. You will need to buy, borrow, or rent a spinning jenny (see illustration, below) to pay out the wire while installing it.

If you are using wooden posts, attach the wires with fencing staples. Do not drive the staples all the way into the posts. Leave enough room for the wire to slide between the wood and the staple. Metal posts should have pre-stamped wire attachment hooks (see illustration, page 37).

Each wire must be tightened; install an in-line wire strainer on each strand (see illustration, right).

*tip*

Posts, wire, and anchors are heavy, and much of their cost comes from shipping. Your best bet is to find local suppliers. Most of them will deliver for a nominal charge. If your new vineyard is large, you may want to consider hiring out the trellis installation part of your project. Fencing contractors have all the tools and supplies to construct a trellis, which is basically a tall fence.

A spinning jenny will save you from hours of aggravation trying to untangle trellis wire. One person sits at the jenny, making sure the wire "pays out" without problem. The other person walks the wire down the vineyard row.

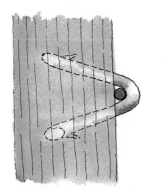 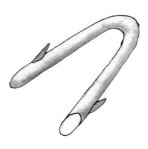

When using wooden posts, use fencing staples to hold the wires in place. Barbed staples hold the best. Most staples are 1 ³/₄" (4.5 cm) long.

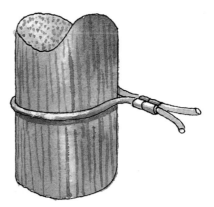

Crimping sleeves are used to attach two pieces of wire, either for slicing purposes or to attach the wires to the end post. Be sure the sleeves are the correct size for 12.5-gauge high-tensile wire. Use a crimping tool to set the sleeves into position.

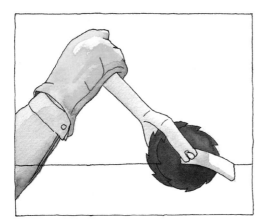

In-line wire tighteners, or strainers, keep wires from sagging. Tighten the wires every spring by cranking the strainer a few times.

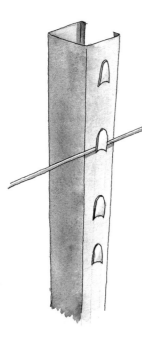

Stamped tabs along the sides of metal posts allow wires to be inserted easily.

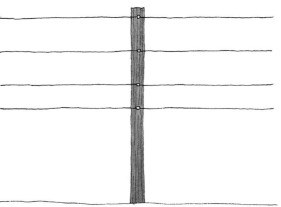

In the vertical shoot positioning (VSP) system, canes are tied to the bottom wire, which is the fruiting wire. The next wire is set about 8" (20 cm) above the fruiting wire, so that you can tie the newly emerged young shoots to the wire before they break in a wind storm or flip downwards from their own weight. Two additional catch wires are usually positioned 12" (31 cm) and 24" (61 cm) above the fruiting wire, so that you can position and tie the shoots to the trellis easily.

# Early
# Vineyard Care

*T*he first growing season is about trellis and training hardware, weed control, and a quick immersion in identifying your native disease and insect populations.

You will not have to do much to your newly planted vines this first year. Most of your time will be spent establishing the trellising. Your goal is to have all posts, anchor and brace assemblies, and at least one wire in place before the vines actively start to grow, which is generally a month or two after planting.

Once daytime temperatures consistently climb above 68°F (20°C), you will see the buds of your newly planted vines swell for a week or so, and then burst open, exposing tender leaves and growing shoot tips (see "Growth Stages of the Vine," page 42). This step is the beginning of the growth cycle. The shoots will grow slowly at first, because the roots are not yet well established. Eventually, depending on your soil's natural fertility and water availability, the shoots will grow more rapidly. About three or four weeks after bud break, the shoots will take off and elongate several inches a week. This stage is when they need to be tied to a stake, or they will grow on the ground where they are difficult to weed, susceptible to disease, and can be stepped on or run over. Try to get vine training stakes in the ground before this happens.

## Training

Training stakes support the young vines and allow the trunks to grow straight. Once your vineyard is three or four years old, the trunks become rigid, and a training stake is no longer needed. Training stakes can be made from various materials, including bamboo (my favorite), wood (such as tomato stakes), metal, and even rigid wire. Stakes should be pushed or pounded into the ground 4" (10 cm) or more, and then tied to the first (fruiting) wire of the trellis (see illustration, right).

Tie your vine's new shoots to the training stake as they elongate. Be sure to tie them loosely—they will expand in diameter, and you don't want to girdle them. The goal is to form a straight trunk and to keep the shoots off of the ground. If the shoots reach the wires, keep tying them upward. Tying materials used at this stage are typically twine, string, or tying tape. (Max Tapener, a Japanese brand-name tying tool, is commonly used and easily available.)

Grape growers have differing opinions on how to best train a vine during the first growing season. Much of their differences relate to how vigorously vines grow from one region to another. In some areas, normal growth might be only 1' or 2' (30.5 to 61 cm) in the first year. Other regions might see 5' or 10' (1.5 to 3 m). Some growers remove all but one or two shoots in the spring. Others pinch off lateral shoots during the growing season to direct growth to the main shoot tip (see illustration, above right). I feel it is best to do nothing but keep the shoots off the ground. And, if you notice grape clusters forming at the bases of the vines when you are working in your vineyard during the summer, I recommend removing them so they don't weaken the young vine. Patience!

## Watering and Fertilizing

If there is little rainfall during the first few months, your newly planted vines will need to be watered. Their roots are trying to establish them-selves, and growing shoots demand lots of water and nutrients. Depending on the size of your planting, manual watering may be sufficient. Larger plantings in dry areas, however, may need permanent soaker hoses or drip irrigation. Be careful not to push your vines by giving them too much water late in the growing season, especially in regions that experience

Newly planted vines should be staked to keep the young, tender shoots off the ground. These shoots will form the vine's permanent trunk, so try to keep them as straight as possible.

Vines not tied to a stake in the first growing season will eventually grow on the ground, making them more susceptible to diseases and damage by tractors and foot traffic.

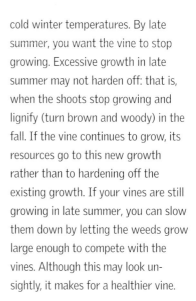

**Tiny grapevine flowers are not particularly attractive, but they are very aromatic.**

cold winter temperatures. By late summer, you want the vine to stop growing. Excessive growth in late summer may not harden off: that is, when the shoots stop growing and lignify (turn brown and woody) in the fall. If the vine continues to grow, its resources go to this new growth rather than to hardening off the existing growth. If your vines are still growing in late summer, you can slow them down by letting the weeds grow large enough to compete with the vines. Although this may look unsightly, it makes for a healthier vine.

## ⬤⬤ Fertilizing

Assuming you have done your homework and have soil tests in hand, you may want to fertilize once the vines are growing. Fertilize your vines only if your agricultural extension agent recommends it (when you get the soil tested) because of specific nutritional deficiencies. Fertilizing young vines may push them too fast.

## Weed Control

Weeds are detrimental to young vines. Newly planted vines do not have much of a root system, and most of their roots are at the soil surface, where weeds compete with them for water and nutrients. To control weeds between the rows, many growers plant grass between the rows. It is easy to maintain (by mowing), looks pretty, and can reduce erosion. The area directly under the vines, however, is more difficult to maintain. Options for weed control directly under the trellis include the following:

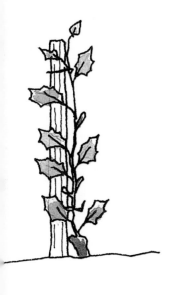

⬤ **Tillage** Tillage includes hand hoeing or using a rototiller. In both cases, it is back breaking work maneuvering around individual vines, especially in wet climates where rainfall encourages rapid weed growth and, in turn, frequent tilling. (Continues on page 44.)

# Growth Stages of the Vine

**Bleeding**  occurs in early spring, and is the stage when the sap starts to flow, but the vines are still dormant. The sap will flow out of pruning cuts, which is perfectly normal and expected. Bleeding begins about a month before bud break and stops after bud break, once the shoots start growing.

**Bud swell**  is when the buds become tender and swollen as they begin to grow inside their sheathing. In some regions, insects such as cutworms and beetles can eat the buds at this stage. Walk your vineyard regularly to look for damage. Bud swell can last for one to three weeks, depending on the temperatures during this stage. Hot temperatures will cause the buds to break quickly (see below). Cool temperatures will delay bud break.

**Bud break**  is when the first green leaves appear—generally happens after the last spring frost (this is what you hope for, anyway) and is the official start of the growing season. Ideally, you want warm spring temperatures during bud break, so that all the shoots begin growing within a few days of each other. Uniformity is always good in a vineyard. Cool temperatures at bud break will result in buds on the same vine breaking over a seven- to ten-day period.

**Early shoot growth**  once temperatures warm, the buds quickly become fast-growing shoots, unfolding leaves and exposing the flower clusters. At this stage, the shoots are tender and can break from high winds or rough handling.

**Flowering**  The period from bud break to flowering (also referred to as bloom) is about fifty days. The vines are self-pollinating, so bees are not necessary, but pollination has a much better chance of success if the weather during flowering is warm and dry. If weather conditions are ideal (warm, sunny, and dry), flowering will be quick (less than a week). If the weather is cool and cloudy, flowering can continue for up to two weeks, which results in berries that begin developing at different times. Uneven berry development can lead to uneven ripening during harvest and is not good for wine quality.

During this stage, and continuing for about one month, the grapes are susceptible to diseases. If the weather in your area at this stage is rainy and humid, fungicide sprays are most important (see disease section [directional]).

**Berry formation**  Tiny berries begin to develop from pollinated flowers within days of "shatter," which is the term for when the flower petals fall off the vine and onto the ground. For roughly fifty days after flowering, the berries grow quickly in size and the shoots continue to lengthen and expand more leaves. This stage is when a lot of canopy management work is required.

## Dormant Bud

Before the warm spring temperatures stimulate growth, the bud is dormant and resistant to cold temperatures

## Bud Swell

At this stage, the bud tissue is still resistant to frost but can be damaged by temperatures below 20°F (−7°C). Insects such as climbing cutworms or flea beetles can also damage the tender buds.

## Bud Break

Once green leaves appear, the emerging shoot is susceptible to frost damage.

*Véraison* is the stage at which red grapes darken and white grapes turn from bright green to an opaque green-yellow. This time is important for the vine; shoot growth should come to a halt now, with all the vine's resources going into ripening the grapes. At véraison, the grapes begin to accumulate sugar and flavors, which is why birds and animals now begin to take an interest in your vineyard.

**Harvest** typically happens anywhere from three to four months after flowering. Harvest decisions will be discussed in-depth in the winemaking section.

**Hardening off** After harvest, the vines need time to harden off and accumulate carbohydrates for the following year. Therefore, you should ensure that the leaves remain healthy, even after harvest. This is when the shoots turn from green to brown.

**Dormancy** When the first hard frost of the fall freezes the vine's leaves, they will quickly fall off of the vine, and the vine enters dormancy. This is a period of rest for the vine—and for the grower (though not the winemaker).

● **Herbicides**   Spraying weed killers around newly established vines must be done with great care, because the herbicide can easily land on vine leaves or green shoots and damage the vine. Some vineyards use milk cartons or "grow tubes" to prevent spray from drifting onto the vines. Never spray in windy conditions. A backpack sprayer—or even better, a spot (also known as sideswipe) applicator—will give you better control.

● **Mulch**   Mulch can suppress weeds, retain moisture, and add organic matter and nutrients to the soil, and it is especially beneficial in dry areas with low-nutrient soils. Pine bark, which breaks down quickly, is ideal. Local availability will dictate what mulch is practical for your vineyard. Black plastic mulch can also control weeds and retain moisture, but it warms up the soil considerably, which can be a problem in hot areas.

On the down side, vine girdling—mice and voles gnawing on vines—can be a problem when mulch is used. To avoid this (the pests make their home under the mulch), keep it a few inches from the base of the vines. Stop using mulch once your vines are older and bearing fruit, because it may add too many nutrients and hold too much water, encouraging excessive vine growth and reducing grape quality.

● **Covercrops**   Low-growing covercrops, such as creeping red fescue or clover, are being used experimentally in high-vine vigor situations. In most cases, however, they are too competitive for young vines.

## Disease Control

Grapevine leaves are susceptible to diseases. Even without grapes on the vines, you need disease-free leaves. Healthy leaves keep the vine growing and developing toward the stage at which it can produce fruit. Two fungus diseases that can attack vine leaves are powdery mildew and downy mildew. I will discuss diseases in more detail in chapter six; for now, however, it is important to know that spraying to prevent mildew needs to start in the first year. Sprays need to be applied preventatively, before disease symptoms become visible. Once you see mildew growing on the leaves, it is too late.

*tip*

When will you see grapes? Vines will produce grapes in the second year, but, except in vigorously growing vineyards, most of these clusters should be removed because they can weaken a young, developing vine. You may want to leave a few clusters, just to taste them in the fall. For winemaking purposes, most vineyards begin to produce a usable amount of grapes in the third year. Again, because the vines are still developing, the crop is usually reduced to a handful of clusters per vine, but this is enough to get started with winemaking. By the fourth year, most vineyards are near full production.

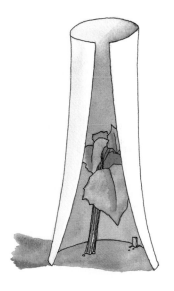

Grow tubes come in various shapes, sizes, and colors and are placed around newly planted vines once the vines show a few leaves. They not only protect the young vines from herbicide drift but also act as training tunnels, promote faster growth, and protect vines in the early stages from predators such as deer.

## Insects

Fortunately, young vines do not suffer from many insect problems. Because insect populations are regionalized, they are difficult to cover in any detail. Unlike disease control, which is preventative, insects need to be controlled only if they are doing substantial damage to the vines. It is a major mistake to spray insecticides indiscriminately, unless you are spraying for a specific pest that you have identified as damaging your vines. This is the basis for integrated pest management (IPM). A complex ecosystem of beneficial and harmful insects exists in your vineyard. Insecticide spray will disrupt this ecosystem and can lead to increased insect problems. You should seek advice on insect control from local resources.

Grow tubes are helpful for much of the first season's growth. They should be removed in the fall, however, especially in regions with cold winters, when their greenhouse effect creates big swings in temperature from day to night. Vines can be damaged by extreme temperature fluctuations in a short period of time.

# Vine Training
# and Pruning

## CHAPTER FIVE

*O*nce your vines begin to grow, you'll need to train them. Vines are extremely malleable and can conform to a vast variety of shapes, systems, and training techniques. Every viticultural region of the world has its own special training system, each adapted to its area's soil, climate, and grape varieties. Many training systems are relatively new. For example, using wires to train vines is a modern concept and has given vineyardists unlimited options. As grapegrowing expanded beyond its traditional European boundaries, new and diverse soils and climates often required more elaborate training systems.

This book concentrates on the basics. Once you understand the terminology, young vine training, and basic cane pruning, you can either keep it simple (as do most of the great grapegrowers of the world) or adapt and change to a system you feel is more appropriate to your situation.

*F*or many wine growers, pruning and training is the most satisfying of all vineyard tasks. You get to know your vines as individuals.

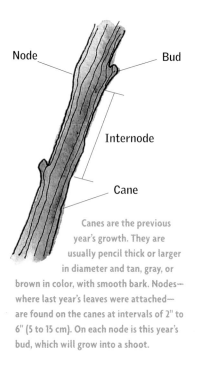

Node

Bud

Internode

Cane

Canes are the previous year's growth. They are usually pencil thick or larger in diameter and tan, gray, or brown in color, with smooth bark. Nodes—where last year's leaves were attached—are found on the canes at intervals of 2" to 6" (5 to 15 cm). On each node is this year's bud, which will grow into a shoot.

Secondary bud

Primary bud

Tertiary bud

The complex bud contains three buds: a primary, which contains most of the flower clusters, a secondary, and a tertiary bud. Generally, only the primary bud grows; if it is damaged by frost or wind, often the less-fruitful secondary or tertiary bud will grow in its place.

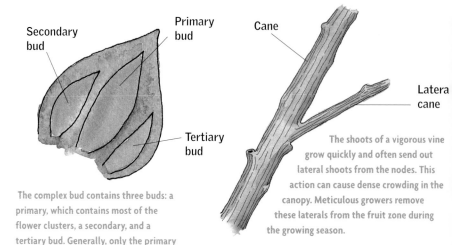

Cane

Lateral cane

The shoots of a vigorous vine grow quickly and often send out lateral shoots from the nodes. This action can cause dense crowding in the canopy. Meticulous growers remove these laterals from the fruit zone during the growing season.

## Terminology

**Bud**   When the vine is dormant, you will see a dark-colored bud at every node. The bud is correctly called a complex bud because it holds three distinct buds—the primary, secondary, and tertiary buds—inside its sheathing. The primary bud is the most important. It will be the first (and usually only) bud to grow and contains most of the grape clusters. If the primary bud is damaged, the secondary or tertiary bud will start growing in its place.

**Cane**   A cane is wood that grew in the previous growing season. It is also known as first-year wood or fruiting cane. Canes are smooth-barked, are about 1/4" to 1/2" (6 to 13 mm) in diameter, and have distinct nodes every 2" to 4" inches (5 to 10 cm). They are typically pruned to a length of six to ten nodes (or buds).

**Head**   At the top of the trunk is the head. It is from this region that canes and spurs originate.

*Young vines ripen their grapes much faster than old vines. The difference can be as much as ten days. There can also be a significant difference in ripening because of soil differences. Thin, well-drained soils ripen grapes faster then heavy, deep soils. This can be true even in the smallest parcels.*

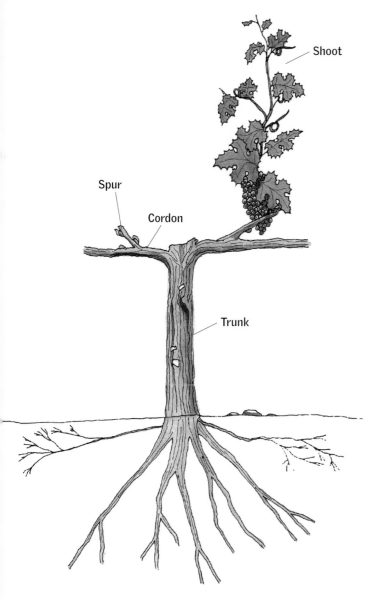

Shoot

Spur

Cordon

Trunk

**Lateral cane**   This is a cane that has grown from the node area of an existing cane. When the vine's roots produce more sap than the main shoot tips can accommodate, they react by pushing out side (lateral) shoots from each node. It indicates excessive vigor and is a sign that the vine is out of balance.

**Node**   The swollen area on a cane where the leaf was attached during the previous growing season. The node is where the bud is located.

**Pruning**   The annual removal of unwanted growth. Pruning maintains the shape of the vine and reduces the following season's crop.

**Spur**   Spurs are canes that are pruned to just one or two buds. In the cane-pruned training system, they are referred to as renewal spurs because shoots that grow from these provide the next season's fruiting canes.

**Sucker/Watersprout**   These are shoots that grew from the trunk or base of the vine during the previous growing season. They are typically removed during that season but are occasionally left to replace damaged or diseased trunks.

**Training**   The process of forming your vines to a specific, permanent system.

**Trunk**   The trunk is permanent. Ideally, once it is established, it will last the life of the vine. It will need support (a training stake) for the first few years, until it becomes rigid. In regions that experience cold winters, it is common practice to train two trunks as insurance against winter damage.

Although popular literature commonly refers to vine roots that plunge deep into the subsoil, most of them are found from 1' to 2' (31 to 61 cm) below the soil. Trunks range in height from less than 1' (31 cm) to more than 6' (2 m), depending on the training system. The left side of this vine shows a permanent arm called a cordon, with a short three-bud spur left after pruning. The right side of the vine shows a shoot actively growing in midsummer with alternating leaves, a grape cluster, and tendrils.

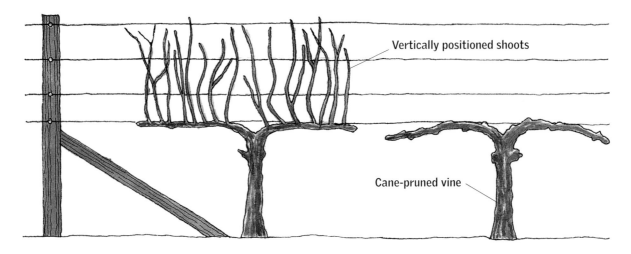

Vertically positioned shoots

Cane-pruned vine

## Forming the Vine

The following training system—called the double Guyot, or cane-pruned VSP (vertical shoot-positioned) system—is the easiest and most common system used worldwide. Once you understand the basics of the Guyot, you can adapt it to various other training techniques (see "Training Variations," on page 53). The following directions take you step by step through each year for an average-vigor vineyard. It is important to note that because of widely varying degrees of vigor, one vineyard's year two may be more like another vineyard's year three. Although I have referred to each stage by year, vines planted in soils with low fertility may take several extra years to reach their final mature stage. Conversely, rich, high-vigor soils may produce large vines that can be cropped in the second year.

### ●● Year One (The Year of Planting)

**Dormant**   If not already pruned at the nursery, prune the vine back to two to four buds before planting.

**Growing Season**   Allow two to four shoots to grow out from the base of the vine. Tie them to a training stake and trellis wire.

### ●● Year Two

**Dormant**   For the trunk, select a cane that is at least the thickness of a pencil. This cane should be straight, not crooked, at the base. Cut (head) the cane about 4" to 8" inches (10 to 20.5 cm) below the fruiting wire. Tie this

The vine on the left shows typical shoot growth during the growing season. This system is commonly referred to as VSP, or vertical shoot positioned. All the shoots grow upwards and are carefully positioned and tied during the growing season. The vine on the right has just been pruned. Two canes have been retained, one on each side.

*V*ines planted in soils with low fertility may take several extra years to reach their final mature stage. Conversely, rich, high-vigor soils may produce large vines that can be cropped in the second year.

# Year One

**Pruning: Dormant Vine**

Dormant vines usually arrive from the nursery already pruned to two to four buds. If not, you should prune them yourself.

**Pruning: Growing Season**

During the first growing season, the vine wants to "bush out," sending out multiple shoots. Some growers remove many of these emerging shoots, preferring to leave only one or two shoots. Or you can let all the shoots grow and save the selection for the following winter's pruning.

# Year Two

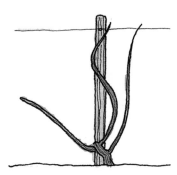

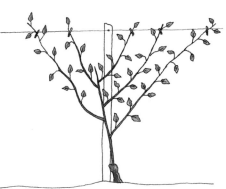

**Pruning:
Dormant Vine, Before Pruning**

This vine shows typical growth after the first year. Three shoots were retained during the growing season. Once their leaves have fallen in the winter, these shoots are then referred to as canes.

**Pruning:
Dormant Vine, After Pruning**

The straightest cane is retained to form the trunk of the vine. This cane is cut, or headed, just below the fruiting wire and tied, to form a straight trunk.

**Pruning:
Growing Season**

During the second growing season, allow four to six shoots to grow from the top of each cane. As these shoots grow, tie them in a fan pattern to the trellis wires.

# Year Three

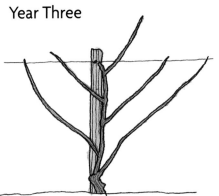

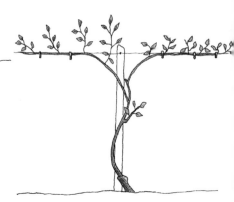

**Pruning:**
**Dormant Vine, Before Pruning**

> By the second winter, the vine will
> have four to six canes. All will be
> candidates for the next season's
> fruiting canes.

**Pruning:**
**Dormant Vine, After Pruning**

> Two canes are selected and tied to the
> fruiting wire. A short renewal spur has
> also been left to provide a well-
> positioned fruiting cane, should it be
> needed next year.

**Pruning:**
**Growing Season**

> In the third growing season,
> depending on the vigor of your
> vineyard, you can allow up to
> ten shoots to grow. These
> shoots will carry your first crop
> of grapes.

cane snugly to the training stake so that it is straight with no bends. If the
first year's growth is weak, and you have no canes of pencil thickness, cut
the cane back to two to four buds, as you did the first year, and start over.

**Growing Season**   Allow four to six new shoots from the head area to
grow. Remove the other lower shoots when they are tender (2" to 6" [5 to
15 cm] long). Tie the young shoots to the catch wires in a rough fan
arrangement, so that they are well exposed to the Sun. For high-vigor
vines, you may leave one cluster of grapes per strong shoot.

## ●● Year Three

**Dormant**   Select two canes from the head area, one on each side. Prune
them back to approximately 12" to 18" (30.5 to 46 cm). Remove all other
canes. Tie the two selected canes to the fruiting wire.

**Growing Season**   Allow four to six shoots to develop from each cane.
Tie them to the catch wires. When clusters appear, leave one cluster per
shoot. This should be your first real harvest year.

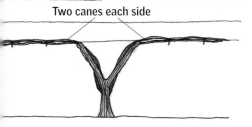

Two canes each side

## Double Canes

To increase the number of shoots—and, in turn, clusters—per vine, leave two canes per side. This is commonly done with small-clustered varieties, whose vines require more shoots to achieve a larger number of clusters.

re

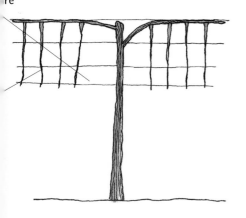

## High-Wire Training

High-wire training works best with varieties that naturally grow downward. Winter pruning is similar to a VSP system, but during the growing season, the shoots are allowed to grow downward.

### ● ● Year Four and Subsequent Years

**Dormant** .Select two canes from the head area, one on each side. Prune them back to a length that will give you six to eight buds per cane. If the selected canes have begun to climb (extending too high or too far away from the head), you may want to leave a one- or two-bud renewal spur along the trunk, below the fruiting cane. This spur is strategically placed to maintain the shape of the vine, so that next year's fruiting canes can be selected from the shoots that originate from this renewal spur, and all other canes are removed.

**Growing Season**   At this point, you have mature vines, so it's time to refer to the section on canopy management in the next chapter

## Training Variations

**Multiple Trunking**   In regions that experience cold winters, I recommend training several trunks of varying ages. Younger trunks are better able to withstand the severe winter temperatures that can sometimes damage older trunks.

**Double Canes**   To increase the number of buds, shoots, and in turn, harvest, some growers will prune to a total of four canes. This method is done primarily with varieties that produce small clusters. Riesling, Gewürztraminer, and most of the Native American vines, for example, have tiny clusters. To produce enough yield, you will need to leave many more buds and shoots per vine. Each shoot usually produces only one or two clusters.

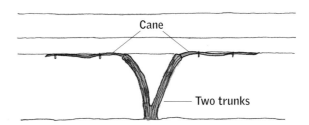

Cane

Two trunks

## Multiple Trunking

In grapegrowing regions in which cold weather can cause winter damage, double trunking is recommended. Retain two canes from the base of the vine; these will eventually form two separate trunks.

**High Wire Training**   Most grapevine varieties have an upright growth habit; that is, their shoots naturally grow upward. However, Native American vines tend to have a procumbent growth habit—their shoots tend to grow downward. For this reason, their fruiting canes are often trained to a high wire (5' to 6" [1.5 to 2 m] from the ground, allowing their shoots to grow downward. This training system is also referred to as a "curtain."

**Cordon/Spur Training**   Instead of renewing fruiting canes every year, the cordon/spur system leaves permanent wood (really a horizontal extension of the trunk) on the fruiting wire. Every year, the canes that grow from the cordons are pruned back to two bud spurs, from which two new shoots arise. This system can be desirable because of its lower yields (that is, the basal buds left for spur pruning are less fruitful—good for large-clustered varieties such as Seyval, Vidal, and some clones of Chardonnay, where the potential crop is always too big and requires time-consuming hand-thinning to avoid taxing and overcropping the vine.

## ●● Divided Canopy Systems

These training systems are involved and are designed for vigorous vines. I don't recommend them for the novice grower, but if your vineyard site proves to be excessively vigorous, you might keep them in mind. You can convert the simple cane-pruned system to one of these later.

The Lyre and Geneva Double Curtain systems are known as horizontally divided canopies. The Scott Henry and Smart-Dyson systems are vertically divided.

- **Lyre System**   The Lyre system is popular in regions in which vine growth is vigorous. The split canopy is a way of spreading out the shoot growth from individual vines.

- **Geneva Double Curtain**   The Geneva Double Curtain is especially popular with large-scale commercial growers, because it adapts well to mechanical pruning and harvesting.

- **Scott Henry System**   The Scott Henry system forms two distinct canopies, one growing up, the other down.

- **Smart-Dyson System**   The Smart-Dyson training system is similar to the Scott Henry, except that it has shoots growing both up and down from the same cane or cordon.

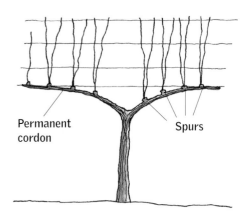

**Permanent cordon**

**Spurs**

## Cordon/Spur Training

Cordon/spur training retains permanent arms called cordons on both sides of the trunk. On each cordon, small spurs, each containing one or two buds, will produce new shoots that grow up the trellis wires and carry that season's grapes.

4' (122 cm)

## Lyre

# *Evaluating Vigor*

When discussing vine growth, I often refer to "balance": balancing your vine's root capacity with the canopy or shoot capacity. The roots supply water and nutrients to the vine. If the roots are well established and the soil has lots of water and available nutrients, lots of sap flows up through the trunk into the growing shoots. In this situation, the vine should have lots of shoots and grapes to take advantage of all that sap flow. If the vine's roots are not well established and water or nutrients are lacking, you will have less sap and corresponding shoot growth will be weaker.

If the previous season's growth is weak—the canes are less than pencil thickness in diameter and shorter than 2' (61 cm)—you have probably allowed too many shoots to grow. Leave fewer buds and shoots when pruning.

If your vines show excessive vigor—canes more than 6' (2 m) long, with large diameters (more than 5/8" [15 mm]) and excessive lateral development and growth—you need to leave more buds and shoots for the coming year, to balance the vigor of your vines.

If your vines are young and still in the training stage, evaluating the shoot growth of the previous season will help you decide how many buds or shoots to leave for the coming season. If your vines are mature (four years or older), evaluating last season's growth will indicate whether you should leave more buds or even canes (see Double Canes, in the next section).

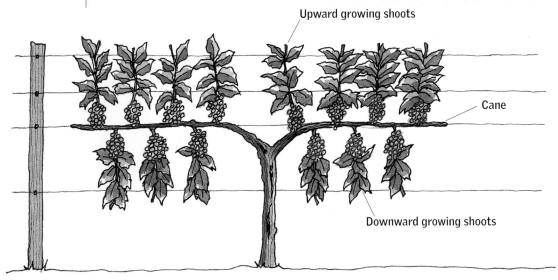

Smart-Dyson

# Taking Care of
# Your Vineyard

## CHAPTER SIX

*E*verything we do during the growing season is aimed at guiding the vine to produce healthy, flavorful grapes so we can make great wine. The vine's leaves are the key. Healthy, well-exposed leaves are the factories that produce all the sugars and flavors that eventually become wine. During the summer, your job is to position the leaves so that they have the best exposure to sunlight. This task is really the whole basis of canopy management.

These leaves need to be healthy. During the critical four to six weeks before harvest, a healthy, well-exposed canopy can do the best job of turning sunlight into wine. The leaves also need to ward off the many diseases and insects that will take interest in both the leaves and the clusters. Every region has a different set of challenges when it comes to keeping vines healthy. We will look at some of the major ones.

*A*ll the small vineyard details—sun exposure, disease prevention, yield—will eventually be accounted for in your wineglass.

# Canopy Management

Before we get into the nitty-gritty of canopy management, we need to understand why we are doing all this work.

Each shoot on a vine should be considered an individual. The leaves on this shoot will provide most of the sugars and flavors for the cluster(s) of grapes attached to it. The ideal shoot will have about fifteen healthy leaves, enough to ripen one average-sized grape cluster (5 to 8 ounces [140 to 225 grams]) or two small ones.

To make fine wine, we must have a uniform canopy. All the shoots should have about the same number of leaves and all should be equally well exposed to the Sun. Each shoot should also carry about the same number of clusters. If one shoot has two large clusters and another has one small one, for example, the ripening will be uneven, leading to a harvest of grapes at many different stages of ripeness. This uneven ripeness can be acceptable for white-wine grapes, but it is a big negative for red-wine grapes, because tannin ripeness must be uniform for optimum quality (see chapter eleven).

Canopy management also includes crop control. Many grape varieties want to overcrop, that is, they want to produce more grapes than can ripen well. If the crop is excessive, the wine quality will suffer. Overcropped vines typically produce wines that are thin and light and lack character. As a rule of thumb, I suggest you aim for a yield of about 1 to 1½ lbs. of grapes per linear foot (1.5 to 2 kg/m) of canopy. In other words, if you have 100' (30.5 m) rows, 100 to 150 lbs. (45.5 to 68) of grapes would be a good-quality yield. It is easy to get higher yields; in fact, reducing yields requires work. Your goal is to have a canopy that is uniform, thin, and open to sun, air flow, and spray coverage.

The following techniques have proven to produce the best wines possible from a given site. They also give us the best tools to manage the fungus diseases and winter hardiness concerns that can be an issue for some regions.

## ●● Shoot Thinning

In the spring, when shoots reach 4" to 8" (10 to 20 cm) long, you may find that some areas of the vine are dense with shoots, whereas other areas are fine. You may see many shoots growing along the trunk and in the head area. These shoots, called watersprouts, usually do not bear any clusters.

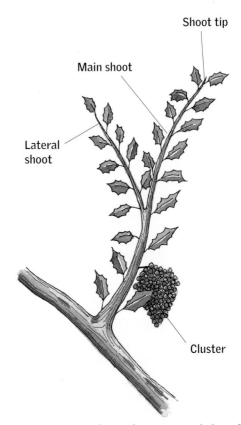

**Shoot tip**

**Main shoot**

**Lateral shoot**

**Cluster**

Grape clusters always appear at the base of a shoot. The leaves above provide the flavors that determine wine quality and style. The side shoot, called a lateral shoot, can also contribute to ripening unless the canopy is too dense and already full of leaves. In this case, laterals only make the canopy more dense and can reduce grape quality by shading.

**Before shoot trimming**

**After shoot trimming**

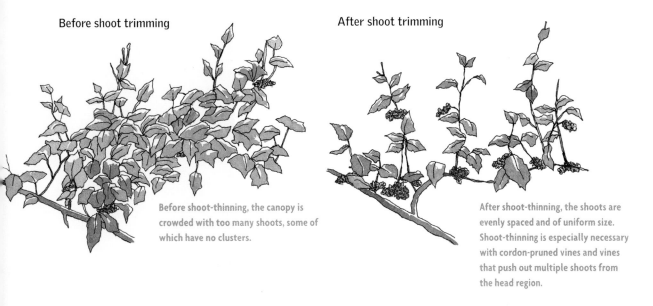

Before shoot-thinning, the canopy is crowded with too many shoots, some of which have no clusters.

After shoot-thinning, the shoots are evenly spaced and of uniform size. Shoot-thinning is especially necessary with cordon-pruned vines and vines that push out multiple shoots from the head region.

However, they take up valuable space on the trellis and should be removed. You may also have more than one shoot coming from a node. Too many shoots can cause crowding; undesirable shoots should be removed early in the season to maintain a uniform, light-penetrating canopy.

The goal is to remove the following:

- shoots at the base and trunk that will not be used for trunk renewal (suckering)

- unfruitful shoots (unless retained for future cane or spur renewal)

- downward-growing shoots

- shoots from excessively dense areas in the canopy; look for a density of two to four shoots per foot of trellis, depending on the variety, vigor, and desired yield. Shoot thinning, after pruning, is our second crop-reduction technique.

## ● ● Shoot Positioning and Tying

After thinning, the shoots grow quickly. As they lengthen, you will need to secure them to the trellis wires. To maintain a uniform canopy, make sure the shoots grow upward, and then tie them to the wires. You can use

When cane pruning, each retained cane needs to be tied to the fruiting wire. This can be done during or after pruning, but it needs to be completed before bud swell, or the tender, swollen buds will be knocked off easily. Tying should be done several times throughout the growing season. Timing is important: Try to tie up shoots just as they start to bend away from the trellis wires. If you wait too long, the canopy becomes a jungle, and the process takes a lot longer.

simple twine for tying, but many horticultural suppliers offer alternatives. My favorite is the Max Tapener tool, which wraps a lightweight tape around the shoot and wire, then cuts and staples it to form a ring that holds the shoot to the wire.

## ● ● Leaf Pulling

About ten days after the vine flowers, it may be a good idea to remove (by hand) some of the leaves around the forming clusters. The goal is to open up the area around the clusters for good air flow (drying), some sun penetration, and spray coverage. Remove the leaves right in the cluster zone, unless you live in a hot growing region, in which case you should retain the leaves on the south and west side (north and west side in the Southern Hemisphere) of the cluster to prevent too much sun falling directly on the grapes (they can get sunburned).

The timing, intensity, and frequency of leaf pulling depend on grape variety, rainfall, and vine vigor. In high-rainfall regions and vintages, leaf pulling is usually very aggressive, because it is important to let the clusters dry out after rain or dew. By removing the leaves in the fruiting zone, air circulates easily and dries the grapes quickly, which is especially important with rot-prone varieties such as Riesling, Sauvignon Blanc, Pinot Noir, and Seyval.

## ● ● Hedging

Hedging is the trimming of the tops and sometimes sides of the vines during the growing season to remove excess growth. It is similar to the trimming you perform on the hedge in your yard. Hedging begins once the shoots attain their maximum desired length (typically 4' to 5' [122 to 152 cm], or twelve to fifteen leaves per shoot). I like to hedge once the shoots have grown about 18" (45.5 cm) above the top trellis wire. At this point, they are usually still upright and easy to clip with hedging shears. You will want to hedge before the vigorous shoots get top heavy and start to fall back down into the canopy. If your vineyard is high vigor, you may need to hedge several times a season as the vine continues to put out new growing tips. In a low-vigor vineyard, one light hedging may be all that is needed.

*tip*

If the leaves in certain sections of your vineyard start to turn dull yellow or even bronze, you could have a mite problem. Mites suck the sap out of the leaves. Dormant oil sprays applied just before bud break may be a good precaution, but avoid using insecticide sprays unless the problem is severe; insecticides also kill predator insects that eat mites.

This canopy looks picture-perfect, in terms of shoot positioning and leaf pulling. The crop, however, is very large, and the wine quality might have been improved with some more judicious cluster-thinning. Ideally, the clusters should be spaced so that none touches another.

## ●● Cluster Thinning/ Green Harvest

Cluster thinning is an emotionally difficult thing to do. You need to remove developing clusters so the vine can better ripen the remaining ones. Usually done just before or during *véraison* (mid-July to mid-August), removing excess clusters prevents overcropping of the vine and helps eliminate less-ripe clusters. Overcropped vines produce lesser-quality wine and are more susceptible to winter damage and decline because they put their energy into ripening the large crop, instead of storing energy for next season's growth. A good rule of thumb is to retain one cluster on any shoot that has ten or more leaves.

Young, drought-stressed, or low-vigor vines often have to be thinned early in the season, just after flowering, so that cluster formation does not compete with vine vigor. I prefer to wait as long as possible with healthy, mature vines. I have found that if the clusters are removed just before or during *véraison*, berry size is smaller, and smaller berries mean less-compact clusters and less rot. (Tight, compact clusters in which all the berries touch one another can result in big rot problems. If there is rot on one berry, it quickly spreads throughout the cluster.) Cluster thinning at *véraison* also offers a particular advantage for red-fruited grape varieties, because visually greener clusters are easier to see and can be removed to achieve a more uniform ripening.

*Warning* Reading this section can be depressing. I'll be discussing almost every problem possible to encounter in the vineyard. Fortunately, no one encounters all of them. With experience in understanding the problems most critical to your situation, you will manage just fine.

The first grape grower's meeting I ever attended was an all-day session on diseases and insects. I was devastated. How could anybody actually grow grapes under such conditions? We can, and in fact, over the past few decades, it has become much easier as we better understand disease and insect cycles and better control tools become available.

## Vine Health

Diseases, insects, and animals large and small will take an interest in your vines. What you may have to contend with largely depends on the location of your vineyard. What can be a major problem for one region may not exist in another area. This is why I highly recommend talking to your local agricultural extension agents and fellow grape growers.

### ●● Diseases

The most problematic diseases for grapevines are fungus diseases, which include mildews and rots that grow on both leaves and fruit and thrive in warm, wet conditions. In humid regions such as northern Europe and eastern North America, controlling disease accounts for a significant amount of the time you spend taking care of your vines. In the drier Mediterranean Europe and western North America, disease control is much easier.

To control fungus diseases, your two best tools are good canopy management, which allows leaves and grapes to dry quickly after a dew or rain, and protective fungicide sprays. You will need to spray your vines on a regular basis to protect them from infection. Once you see the disease, it is too late. I'll look at the four major grapevines diseases first and then discuss strategies to control them.

**Powdery Mildew** A universal problem, powdery mildew is the one fungus disease that does not need water or humidity to grow (it grows well in both wet and dry conditions). Powdery mildew can develop on the

Powdery mildew at first looks like a light grayish-white dust on the top side of the leaves or in the clusters. As it matures, it dries out the leaves and splits the grapes.

Downy mildew is usually a leaf problem. It can damage young leaves and even defoliate vines if it gets out of hand. Some grapes are also susceptible to downy mildew, especially in the month or so after flowering.

Symptoms of black rot are distinctive brown lesions on the leaves. Infected grapes will quickly turn black, dry out, and turn into "mummies" that stay intact on the clusters.

Botrytis rot is identified by distinct gray "fuzz" in its early stages. The grapes slowly dry out but have sweet, attractive flavors.

vine's leaves throughout the growing season, especially when it is hot. If left unchecked, it will eventually kill the affected leaves and defoliate the vine. Even mildly infected leaves will not photosynthesize well, which results in poorly ripening grapes. The grapes themselves are also susceptible to infection when they are in the development stage, from flowering until véraison. The most common and effective protective spray is sulfur, which is inexpensive and widely available. Sulfur is usually sprayed every ten days, starting when the shoots are 10" (25 cm) long, up to thirty days before harvest.

**Downy Mildew**　Downy mildew is a problem in wet growing areas, where heavy morning dews and regular rainfall during the growing season are the norm. Persistent rains, especially those that leave the canopy wet overnight, are the worst culprits. Young leaves are most easily infected. Fortunately, most grape varieties are resistant to cluster infections. Copper, Captan, and Mancozeb are the most common and effective protective fungicides available to control downy mildew. Labeling and local restrictions can apply to these products. Read the labels carefully. Typically they are sprayed every ten days and are mixed and sprayed with sulfur.

**Black Rot**　Also exclusively found in humid grape growing areas, black rot likes the same conditions as downy mildew. Although it does infect the leaves, foliar damage is minimal—the real problem is with the young grape clusters. From flowering and for the subsequent four or five weeks, the young, developing grapes are highly susceptible to black rot, especially if this period is wet. Again, Copper, Captan and Mancozeb are effective protective fungicides. Follow the recommendations for downy mildew.

**Bunch Rots**　Bunch rots occur during wet harvests. If the period after véraison—and especially just before harvest—is rainy, some grape varieties (especially the white-fruited ones) can succumb to bunch rots. There are two general types of bunch rots: botrytis rot and sour rot. Botrytis bunch rot, a distinctive gray mold, grows on the grapes' skins. If the grapes are ripe when botrytis attacks, it can actually be a good thing for the winemaker. Many of the greatest dessert wines are made from botrytis-infected grapes.

Sour rot is an entirely different story. Unlike botrytis, which is one specific fungus, sour rot can be caused by a number of organisms, both fungi and bacteria, that attack susceptible grape varieties and turn them to vinegar. These organisms are opportunistic, looking for wounds (insect damage), cracks, or breaks (microscopic splitting from the swelling after a big rain) in the skin. They then grow and multiply within the cluster. If your harvest season is warm and humid, avoid planting susceptible varieties, such as Riesling, Pinot Gris, Sauvignon Blanc, Pinot Noir, and Seyval. Instead, try more rot-resistant varieties such as Vidal, Cabernet, Chardonnay, and most of the Native American varieties.

The best way to avoid problems with bunch rots is by practicing good canopy management, especially leaf pulling around the clusters. Specific botrytis sprays are commercially available, but they are expensive and of limited efficacy.

## ●● Spraying

Regardless of which grape varieties you grow or where you grow them, you will need to spray your grapes. Because each region of the world has its specific disease pressures and problems, I strongly suggest acquiring your own state, province, or county spray recommendations and following them. General-purpose fruit sprays are available at most garden supply centers; they will probably work most of the time, especially when your vines are young. You are better off, however, getting more specific recommendations for your area. It is environmentally and personally unhealthy to spray needlessly.

## ●● Insects

Fortunately, insect damage is much easier to deal with than diseases. With insects, you can wait for the damage to appear and then decide if the damage is significant enough to require spraying. Many insects feed on grapevines, but only occasionally will their populations be high enough and the damage severe enough for insecticide use. Insects can damage grapevines in three ways.

- **Buds** Bud swell in the early spring attracts cutworms and beetles, which eat the tender buds.

Detailed disease and insect spray recommendations can be found online in almost every state, province, and region. Use your search engine to find your regional agricultural university; the relevant information is often listed under "small fruits."

There are many species of leafhoppers. All species suck the sap out of leaves. If the damage becomes too great (the leaves begin to yellow), you may have to spray. Some species of leafhoppers can also transmit diseases such as Pierce's Disease and Grapevine Yellows. In this case, control measures need to be increased.

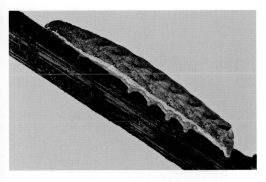

The climbing cutworm spends the day in the soil around the base of the vine. It emerges at night, climbs the trunk, and eats the swollen buds. It takes only one cutworm to eat most of the buds on one vine. If you see damage to your newly swollen buds, you may want to walk your vineyard at night and eliminate feeding cutworms.

The larva of the grape berry moth is one of several insects that burrow into grape berries and eat the insides. The problem is not so much the loss of the individual berries but the resulting rot, which can spread throughout the entire cluster.

Unchecked, they can destroy enough buds in as little as a day or two to significantly reduce your potential crop. Walking your vineyards daily is recommended. If the damage comprises more than ten percent of the buds, insecticide spray may be necessary.

- **Leaves** Throughout the growing season, insects will be interested in your grapevine's leaves. In most cases, the damage is obvious and slow, as large populations of caterpillars or beetles, such as Japanese beetles (eastern United States) or the grapeleaf skeletonizer (western United States), for example, descend on the vines annually. Grapevines, especially high-vigor vines, can take a fair amount of leaf loss by insects. Don't run for your sprayer just because you see a few caterpillars. Evaluate the damage they are doing, then make your decision.

  Other insects, such as leafhoppers and mites (mites are not really considered insects because they have eight legs), can cause more subtle vine damage as they slowly and inconspicuously suck the sap from the leaves. Over time, the leaves turn slightly yellowed or bronzed. To add insult to injury, certain species of leafhoppers can transmit diseases such as Pierce's disease, a bacteria that can kill susceptible varieties and is currently a problem in southern California, or Grapevine Yellows, which affects vines in Europe, Australia, and the eastern United States.

- **Fruit** Insects that feed on the grape berries are usually the most damaging, not only because of the obvious reduction in crop but also because of the consequent rot that the damaged berries can spread throughout the entire cluster. Most viticultural regions have to contend with one species of larva that drills into the berry and feeds on the interior. Every area of the world seem to have a different version of a similar problem. Protected inside the berry, these larvae are difficult to control using sprays. New developments in pheromone mating disruption have resulted in the introduction of nonchemical deterrents to some species, but carefully timed insecticide sprays are still the norm.

## Spraying Tips

- Most fungicide sprays are protective, meaning they need to be applied before the disease becomes active and certainly before you see any signs of the disease. This often means spraying just before a rain (the wetness from the rain is what triggers the disease). Spraying before a rain may seem counter-intuitive—you expect the spray to wash off—but it is considered to be the best timing.

- The most critical times to spray are from bloom to five weeks past bloom. This is when the clusters are most susceptible to diseases.

- Good coverage is essential. Any fungicide spray must cover all surfaces of the leaves and clusters.

- You can mix several products into one spray tank, but always read the labels to be sure they are compatible.

- Use common sense when spraying. Protect yourself from drift, use a respirator, and avoid spraying when it is windy.

**Spraying for Insects**   Every year, new insecticide formulations are introduced in the marketplace. Less toxic and more insect specific, these formulations are more environmentally friendly than older insecticides, such as Sevin and Malathion, which are broad-spectrum insecticides, meaning they kill a wide number of insect species. The problem with broad-spectrum insecticides is that they kill the "good" insects (predators) as well as the bad (those that attack vines). A classic example is with mites, whose populations often flare up after an insecticide spray. Many insects feed on mites, keeping their populations at acceptable levels. If these predator insects are destroyed, mite damage can often be observed. Newer insecticides target only the problem insect and do less harm to the overall insect population. Of course, these products are more expensive.

*It is a major mistake to spray insecticides unless you are spraying for a specific pest that you have identified as damaging to your vines.*

## *Phylloxera*

Phylloxera is a tiny insect that lives in soil and feeds on the roots of grapevines. It is native to the eastern United States, where native grapevines evolved with phylloxera and are somewhat resistant to its damage. The phylloxera, however, can quickly devour he roots of the European *Vitis vinifera*. In the mid-1800s, horticulturists from Europe imported Native American vines for research and collections. Unfortunately, phylloxera went along for the ride. The insect quickly spread throughout most of Europe and destroyed the grape and wine industry.

The Europeans eventually found two methods to deal with this new pest: They grafted their susceptible vines onto resistant American rootsock and they hybridized the European varieties with resisant American varieties. The resulting vines are called American hybrids in France and French hybids in America. We'll refer to them as French-American hybrids.

Today, with few exceptions, phylloxera afects most grape growing regions. Standard practice is to plant grafted *vinifera* vines, French-American hybrids, or Native American vines, all of which are resistant to phylloxera damage.

### ● ● Birds

Birds are a major problem in some areas. Just a few pecks in a grape berry can initiate rot damage, but in some cases, the birds are so voracious that there are no berries left to rot. If you find birds to be a problem, netting is probably the only deterrent. Netting is usually placed over each individual row and then tied or secured at the base of the canopy. If your damage is only moderate, scare devices, ranging from "cannons" that blast loud, gunlike sounds to computerized recordings that sound like birds being tortured, can be effective. (Your neighbors will love you.) If your bird pressure is light, using reflective metallic polyester tape and scare balloons may be deterrent enough.

### ● ● Mammals

Deer, raccoons, kangaroos, wild boars, bears: you name it, they all love grapes. Every region has its favorite predator and a way to deter it. Fencing is usually the best way to keep out the varmints. Many designs are available, depending on what animal you are trying to keep out. Most are designed for deer, the biggest animal problem in much of the grapegrowing world. If predator populations are moderate, repellents such as hot sauce or rotten eggs sprayed on the vines (but not the fruit, for obvious reasons) may be effective, and some growers swear by home remedies such as hanging human hair or soap around the vineyard.

# Making Wine

Wine is a product of the farm. Soil, weather, grape variety, and the vintner's hand determine the flavors and qualities of the all-important raw ingredient. In a sense, most of the work has been done to get to the point we are at now: turning grapes into wine.

# Getting Started

## CHAPTER SEVEN

*Our goal is to keep the winemaking process as simple as possible. Simplicity often makes the best wines, if we start with good grapes.*

*T*here are as many approaches to wine-making as there are wines. Some winemakers refuse to add anything to their wines, whereas others have no problems with this. Some ferment warm, others cool. Yeast strains, the use of oak, and filtration—all are areas of differing opinions. This is the beauty of wine and its making.

Over the years, I have been on the receiving end of many great words of winemaking wisdom. "Trust your wine" are three words that often come to mind when I am grappling with a winemaking decision. If I am not sure whether I should rack off the lees, add more sulfur, or bottle early, my resulting action is always to do nothing. I am a huge advocate of keeping things simple.

There is a correlation between great wine and the courage to do nothing in the cellar. This concept puts this book and me firmly in the traditional Old World winemaking camp. Let me explain.

Some winemakers believe in a scientific approach (the new-world approach) to making wine, whereby lab analyses and their resulting numbers guide the decision-making process. Acid levels, pH, and sugar percentages are measured and adjusted accordingly; concentrates, enzymes, tannins, and other amendments are added—in an effort to theo-retically improve the wine. This is commonly referred to as "making wine by numbers."

Wines made the scientific way are often easy drinking and pleasant. But they can lack character and soul. They do not have a sense of place or personality. Some cynics refer to these wines as "Frankenstein wines," comparable to elevator music.

The Old World approach is based on making the wine in the vineyard. All the quality decisions discussed in the previous chapters about grape-growing are meticulously implemented. In this sense, the wine makes itself, with little intervention after harvesting from the winemaker. This noninterventionist winemaking philosophy is similar to the approach used by great chefs who scour the markets each day for the freshest ingredients and use minimal seasonings and sauces in their simple, but flavorful, cuisine.

Wines made by the noninterventionist technique are not perfect. In fact, that is not the goal. These wines often need bottle aging because they have lots of edges and imperfections that harmonize with time. They can be compared to singer-songwriters. They might not have perfect pitch, but they are passionately moving. Character, personality, and a sense of place define these wines. *Terroir* is the French term that best describes this. The word has no English equivalent. I define *terroir* as the place in which the grapes are grown reflected in the personality of the wine. It's what makes your wine unique.

> *Character, personality, and a sense of place define these wines. Terroir is the French term that best describes this.*

## Les Garagists

*Les garagists* is a French term that describes small-scale, progressive wine-makers who have very basic facilities but make outstanding wines. The movement started in Bordeaux in the 1980s and has spread worldwide. Les garagists—winemakers who break all traditions and spurn the idea that one needs millions of dollars to start a quality winemaking facility—make world-class wines in their garages (or similarly sized facility). Many of the wines are among the most sought after in the world. Production is often only a few barrels. The point is that having lots of space and equipment is great, but the grapes and the person making the decisions are what really count.

A true garagist at work. Harvesting, crushing, and pressing are always sticky affairs and will permanently stain your clothes.

# Making Wine—An Overview

Winemaking can be a simple process. In fact, my goal is to keep it as simple as possible. Simplicity often makes the best wines, if we start with good grapes. Let's get acquainted with the basic steps of winemaking before we plunge into the details. Many variations of the process exist, as you will see in the following chapters.

Following are the major steps in the winemaking process, for white winemaking and for red winemaking. (You may find it helpful to refer to the Glossary, page 166.)

## ●● White Winemaking

After harvest, white-wine grapes are placed immediately into the press. (In some cases, white grapes are carefully crushed first, to help release the juice.) The juice is transferred to a glass carboy (racking), where gravity settles out some of the small pieces of skin and pulp (the lees). After the clear juice is siphoned off into a different carboy, yeast is added and fermentation begins. Fermentation of white wines lasts from one to four weeks. After fermentation stops, the new wine is racked again, into another carboy, and aged, before bottling.

## ●● Red Winemaking

Red grapes are lightly crushed, destemmed, and placed into an open vat. Yeast is added, and the crushed grapes ferment in contact with their skins. During fermentation, the skins are manually mixed with the fermenting juice (punching down). Once fermentation slows, and the juice tastes more like red wine, the contents of the fermenter are poured into a press, where the wine is separated from the skins. After settling overnight, the wine is racked into a carboy or barrel for aging.

# Your Space

Wines have been made for centuries without running water, electricity, or refrigeration. Some of the best wines I have ever tasted came from facilities that were bare-bones.

In deciding where to make wine, you'll need to consider the three distinct phases involved in winemaking: crush, fermentation, and cellaring.

## ●● Crush

Crushing—when you unload the grapes, sort them, crush them, and press out the juice—is the messy part. You have lots of stems and skins to dispose of. Everything is sticky from juice. Washing down is an integral part of this process, and you will need lots of space that can be easily cleaned: perhaps, your backyard, or even your driveway. A covered area such as a garage or basement is better in case it rains or to keep the hot sun off of you and the grapes. Your most important tool is a garden hose for rinsing. Hot water is a big plus but is not absolutely necessary.

## ●● Fermentation

Where you ferment depends on whether you are making red or white wines. Red wine fermentation is done at higher temperatures (70°F to 80°F [21°C to 27°C]), needs daily attention, and attracts lots of fruit flies. A warm garage or kitchen is ideal. White wines usually ferment cooler (ideally 50°F to 60°F [10°C to 15°C]) and are quite happy being left alone fermenting for weeks at a time, except for the occasional sniff or taste. A cool basement or unheated garage (late fall only, once the air temperatures drop) would work.

## ●● Cellaring

Cellaring includes aging and, eventually, bottling the wine. Again, temperature is important. Wines age best in a cool environment between 50°F and 62°F (10°C and 17°C). Heat is especially damaging to wines, so avoid spaces in which temperatures exceed 72°F (22°C). If you store wines in glass, a dark space is preferable—a cellar is ideal.

A perfect situation would be to crush outside or in a garage, ferment reds in a warm garage and whites in the cool cellar, then age all the wines

*... True quality is that which succeeds in surprising and moving us. It is not locked inside a formula. Its essence is subtle (subjective) and never rational. It resides in the unique, the singular, but it is ultimately connected to something more universal. A great wine is one in which quality is contained. Such a wine will necessarily be uncommon and decidedly unique because it cannot be like any other, and because of this fact it will be atypical, or typical only of itself.*

*— Andre Ostertag*

in the cool cellar. If you don't have the perfect situation, you will most likely have to compromise. Some home winemakers, for example, use a refrigerator as their "cool cellar" or leave the wines outside at night, if the temperatures are cool enough.

## Tools of the Trade

It is easy to become overwhelmed by the vast array of available wine-making equipment, tools, and gadgets. Here, too, you can compare wine-making to cooking. I have been told that the most important tools a chef needs are good knives, good pans, and an unlimited supply of clean towels. Sometimes the basics are all that is really needed. This book is geared toward minimalist winemaking, in terms of winemaker intervention as well as equipment. I suggest not purchasing a new tool or piece of equipment until you are really sure that you need it. You want to keep this adventure affordable.

### ●● Crushers

Crushing is the process of gently extracting juice or wine from grapes. It is possible to do this entire process manually, using your feet or hands. However, with certain pieces of equipment, you can lessen the workload and extract more juice from your grapes.

Crushers can be operated manually (using a hand crank) or motorized. Whole clusters of grapes are dropped into a hopper and are squeezed between two serrated rollers, which lightly break the skins ("crush" is a misnomer) to release the juice. When making red wines, the crusher is placed over a vat or bucket, which becomes the fermenter. When making whites, the crusher is placed directly over either the press or a bucket, and the crushed grapes are poured into the press.

A crusher is not really needed for making white wine, although crushing white grapes makes the pressing process (in which you actually squeeze out the juice) more efficient. Crushed grapes release juice easily; whole grapes have to be popped by the pressure of the press. You do need to crush when making red wine. Crushing red grapes helps extract the skin's flavors, tannins, and color, which develop as the juice ferments.

**This hand-operated crusher will break open the grape skins for easier juice extraction.**

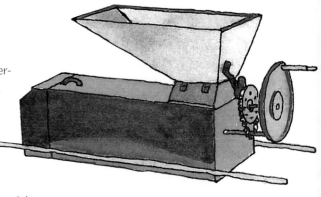

##  Destemmers

Motorized crushers are commonly fitted with a destemmer, a spherical cage with holes large enough for grape berries, but not stems, to fall through. As the cage rotates, a series of small beaters, called fingers, rotate in the opposite direction, detaching the grape berries from their stems. The berries fall through the holes, whereas the stems are pushed, or augured, to the end of the cage, where they fall to the ground. No destemmer is 100 percent efficient, even the big, expensive, commercial ones. Small stem fragments, known as jacks, break off during the process and fall through the holes along with the berries. Fastidious red winemakers often pick out these jacks by hand, because they can contribute a bitter taste to the wine.

The crusher/destemmer both breaks the skins and removes most of the stems. It is especially recommended for red wine production.

## The Press

The press is where you probably want to put your money. It is the time-tested way of squeezing juice or wine out of the grape. You can get by without a press by using your hands and pressing the grapes in a colander, but this method is much less efficient, in terms of time and, more important, the amount or juice or wine that you can get from a given quantity of grapes. The most common, simple, and least-expensive type of press is a ratchet basket press, which looks very much like a wooden barrel with spaces between the slats. The juice or wine flows through the gaps when pressure is applied by a lid that is slowly ratcheted down on top of the grapes or must. The force comes from either a large screw or by a device that is very similar to a car tire jack.

## Fermentation Vessels

The type of fermentation vessel you use depends on whether you are fermenting red or white wine. Fermenting red grapes need to be punched down or stirred on a regular basis, so you'll need an open-top fermenter—a large bucket will work for small lots. Food-grade plastic tubs or drums cut in half work well for larger quantities. A sheet or cloth is placed on top to keep fruit flies out of the juice. White wines ferment without skins, so there is no need to stir or punch down; large, glass bottles called carboys are the standard fermentation vessel for whites.

This small press is very efficient, especially for pressing red wine. Red wine grape skins and pulp have been broken down by fermentation, leaving fewer solids to squeeze. White wine grapes require more pressing time and patience.

Tubs like this large, red one (above) are not only useful for harvesting grapes, clean tubs can also be used as open-top fermenters.

You'll need a fermentation lock when fermenting in a closed container such as a carboy. Fermenting wines give off quite a lot of carbon dioxide gas ($CO_2$), which must be allowed to escape, or the stopper (also known as a "bung") or container will crack from the pressure. The lock, which has a small amount of water in it, is inserted through a hole in the stopper. During fermentation, the $CO_2$ escapes through the lock—you'll see bubbles in the water—but fruit flies and air cannot pass through in the opposite direction.

## ●● Aging Vessels and Bottling Tools

Minimal equipment is needed during the aging process, which the French refer to as *élevage*. Most home winemakers age their wine in the same glass carboys used to ferment the white wines. Have on hand bottles of varying sizes, ranging from 375 ml to 5 gallons (25 L), so you can accommodate any size batch. The next step up from carboys (a giant leap, really) is the use of oak barrels. Oak barrels are wonderful vessels in which to both ferment and age wine, but they do have some serious drawbacks for the home winemaker. They are very expensive, even the small ones, and when new, they tend to overwhelm the wine with excessive oak flavors. They are also difficult to maintain and prevent from going bad. I will discuss barrels, along with oak chips, in more detail in chapter twelve.

## *Merlot*

In good vintages, Merlot grapes can make dry, rich, supple wines. They are often blended with Cabernet Sauvignons to produce a softer wine. Most Merlots can be consumed when young, but some of the greatest examples of this grape from Pomerol and St. Emilian will improve for decades.

**Taste characteristics:** ripe berries; soft, fruity, supple in texture

**Serve:** 60°F to 65 (15°C to 18°C)

**Pair with:** Grilled red meats, hard cheeses

Have an assortment of bottles on hand, in varying sizes, to accommodate various quantities of wine. These will come in handy when you get to the aging stage.

For bottling, you'll need corks, bottles, and a simple siphon hose. If you use traditional corks, you will need a small hand or floor corker. "Bar top" corks, with plastic tops, can be pushed in manually.

Other basic tools needed in the cellar are scrub brushes and plastic buckets for cleaning, funnels, and, most important, a wine glass!

## ●● Cleaning

Hot water and elbow grease are the best cleaning tools. Try to spray down any area or equipment immediately after you have finished using it. Once juice or wine dries, it is much more difficult to remove. Avoid using detergents or bleach on any surface that comes in contact with juice or wine; they can leave residues that may be absorbed by the juice or wine. Washing soda, also known as sodium carbonate, is highly alkaline and good at removing hard-to-clean wine or juice stains. A potassium metabisulfite (sulfur) solution will help sanitize equipment. You are not going to sterilize anything—sterile means the absence of any micro-organism, which is practically impossible on a home winemaking level. You simply want to reduce population levels. Be sure to clean all your equipment thoroughly before using it, and use new bottles, if possible, for bottling.

## ●● Lab Tests

As much as I try to avoid using science and numbers in winemaking, some basic tests are necessary, and for this you'll need something to serve as a laboratory. Yours can consist of a folding table or the kitchen counter.

Barrels are a luxury for the home winemaker. You need to make a substantial amount of wine before considering using barrels, because of both the volume and the risk of leaving a wine too long in the barrel and overoaking it. It is best to use a small barrel and rotate different wines in and out of it throughout the year.

*T*he most valuable tool for making good wine is your palate. Develop it by going to tastings and buying wine. Taste critically with others who have experience and knowledge. Invest in journals and books. Winemakers who depend on their palates to make decisions produce the best wines at the lowest cost.

Many analyses can be performed on wine. If you fancy yourself a chemist and enjoy this aspect of winemaking, there are volumes written on the subject. However, my philosophy is to train your palate to be your laboratory. In the trade, we refer to this as organoleptic analysis. Sounds impressive, but all it means is that you base winemaking decisions on taste. This approach dovetails well into the scale of the home wine-maker because many of the more advanced analyses are expensive and time consuming.

To get started, you'll need to measure three levels in basic lab tests: the sugar level of the juice, the acid level of the juice and wine (acid levels change after fermentation), and the sulfur dioxide ($SO_2$) level during aging. I will address the sugar and acid tests in chapter eight and the $SO_2$ test in chapter twelve.

Two handy measuring instruments to have are a thermometer and a gram scale.

## ●● Other Supplies

To get started, you will need a few basics. Sulfur dioxide in the form of potassium metabisulfite will be discussed in detail in chapter nine. Its use in winemaking is considered essential to prevent premature oxidation (browning) of wines.

*tip*

A clean working area and good lab analysis will contribute to making a clean, sound balanced wine. If your workspace or cellar is dirty and moldy, or if you skip the lab tests and decide to "just wing it," you could end up with a lot of cooking wine. You could just as easily produce a wine of great character and interest. Winemaking can often surprise you.

# Finding Grapes

The focus of this book is to take you through the entire process, from planting your vines to bottling your wine. Obviously, this takes many years, and most of us are anxious to get started with the winemaking before our own vineyard is producing. A few sources for grapes and grape juice follow. When investigating them, try to stay local, if possible. So much of quality winemaking is reading and reacting to the idiosyncrasies of the vintage, notably the weather influences in the month or so leading to harvest. You can fine tune these instincts if you live in the area in which you buy your grapes.

**Local Wineries** In most grape growing regions of the world, you can find small growers who sell grapes to home winemakers. Your local wineries are a good resource for this; they often know of small, independent grape growers who do not advertise and may sell grapes or juice themselves. For white-wine production, it is possible to buy fresh juice and ferment it at home, but because red grapes need to ferment on their skins, grapes or freshly crushed grapes are the only way to go.

**Gleaning** Gleaning is the ancient practice of scouring the vines after the harvest. In the frenzy of the harvest, grape clusters are often overlooked, especially white-fruited varieties, because their green hue blends in with the leaves and makes them difficult to see. In addition, most vines produce a small crop of secondary grapes that ripen much later than the primary grapes. These are not picked during the main harvest. If the growing season is long enough, they

will ripen, but most commercial vineyards don't bother to harvest them because the quantity is too small to bother with.

Remember that most commercial vineyards are under a lot of stress during harvest. For this reason and for liability concerns, they may not be interested in allowing gleaners in their vines. If you can volunteer to help them out during harvest, it would go a long way in opening some doors.

**Brokers** A number of brokers, especially in cities on the East Coast of the United States, bring in grapes from California for home winemakers. Some are listed in the Resources section (see page 167). They continue the Prohibition-era tradition of supplying Italian immigrants with a necessary staple. As home winemakers become increasingly sophisticated, so do these suppliers, bringing in grapes or even frozen, crushed red grapes from very reputable vineyards.

**Kits** Winemaking kits consist of grape juice concentrates that can be fermented easily and inexpensively into wine. Kits allow you to make wine at any time (you don't have to wait for autumn) and become familiar with the fundamentals of winemaking at minimal cost. However, so much of making fine wine is the satisfaction of understanding your vines, the timing of harvest, and becoming intimate with your grapes. Kits are no substitute for understanding the basics of making great wine, but they can be a good place to start learning from your mistakes.

Carbon dioxide and other inert gas blends are now available in small, affordable quantities. These gases are used to fill a carboy, barrel, or bottle before wine enters them to reduce oxygen pickup. Although not essential, $CO_2$ is very helpful, especially in white-wine production, because white wines are more prone to oxidation than red wines.

You will also need yeasts and yeast food, which will be discussed in more detail in chapter nine.

Finally, as you get further into the nuances of winemaking, you will probably begin experimenting with fining agents. These are mostly natural compounds that are added to a juice or wine to clarify, stabilize, and/or round out the finish. I'll discuss these further in chapters ten and twelve.

There is no true substitute for making wine from your own grapes, but concentrate kits can help you learn some basic concepts while you wait for your vines to mature. Another bonus: Your mistakes will be less expensive.

*In Europe, most wines are identified and labeled with the name of the place in which the grapes were grown, with rarely a mention of the grape varieties in the bottle. In the New World, varietal labeling, or identifying the wine by the grape variety used to make it, is more common. Each case is indicative of the philosophical emphasis of the winegrower.*

# When
# to Pick

## CHAPTER EIGHT

*T*here is a reason that grapes, more than any other fruit, have historically been used in wine-making. No other fruit naturally provides the right amount of sugar, acid, and flavor to produce a balanced wine. Whereas other fruit wines require the addition of cane sugar and other ingredients, ripe grapes that are grown in appropriate climates naturally make fine, balanced wine, with little or no intervention by the winemaker.

In this chapter, we'll learn how to evaluate both the flavor and chemistry of ripening grapes and how to use this information to make picking and winemaking decisions. Sugar, acidity, flavors, and aromas all change as grapes ripen. Some wines are better balanced with more acidity, others with more alcohol (wines fermented from grapes with a higher sugar content). The vintner's challenge is to harvest at optimal maturity for the type of wine being made. When to pick is arguably the most important winemaking decision you'll make.

*E*very day during the ripening season, the grapes change in some way. This is the time of year when the winegrower makes an almost spiritual bond with Mother Nature.

## Evaluating Grape Ripeness

Picking decisions have a lot to do with experience. Each vineyard site and grape variety has its own idiosyncrasies. The Chablis region is usually cool, producing wines from the Chardonnay grape with crisp acidity, whereas the warmer Napa Valley produces Chardonnays that are typically high in alcohol and low in acidity. Weather—hot, cool, wet, dry, sunny, cloudy— plays a major role. This is why wines are vintage-dated. The weather during those last few weeks of ripening is critical in determining the style and quality of your wine. Each year, the wine from the same vineyard will be different, which is why winemakers never get bored.

Most novice winemakers will rely heavily on the numbers: the sugar and acidity levels. With more time and experience, you'll discover that flavor, aroma, and visual indicators play a much more significant role in making picking decisions. We'll take a more in-depth look at these factors in the chapters on white and red winemaking. For now, let's focus on some of the most important basic ripening indicators.

## Sugar

When winemakers refer to sugar measurements, they use the term Brix (pronounced "bricks"). For all practical purposes, Brix is the percentage of sugar in the grape or juice. It's expressed in degrees (as in 23° Brix) but refers to a percentage (23° Brix is 23 percent sugar). The grape's Brix content is traditionally considered the most important measurement of ripeness and quality. Sugar content is important because it is what the yeast ferments into alcohol. The higher the Brix level in the juice, the higher the alcohol level in the resulting wine.

The sugar content in grapes is produced by healthy leaves that are well exposed to abundant sunshine. Diseased leaves, poorly managed canopies, and cloudy weather can all contribute to low grape-sugar levels. A soaking rain in the weeks before harvest will dilute all the components in the grape, including the sugar. This dilution occurs when the roots draw in all the newly available water from the soil and pump it directly into the grapes. In lesser vintages—meaning rainy autumns—natural sugar levels tend to be quite low. However, with global warming and greatly improved vineyard practices, Brix levels seem to be much higher than they used to

### Refractometer

A refractometer measures the sugar or Brix level of juice. It can be carried into the vineyard to check the progress of individual ripening berries or used at home to check the Brix of freshly crushed must.

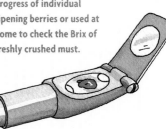

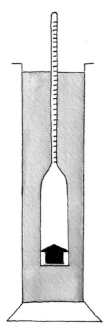

## Hydrometer

A hydrometer is a very accurate, inexpensive method to determine the sugar content of juice and must.

*tip*

To evaluate your ripening grapes, you need to take samples at least once a week. I randomly walk the vineyard with marked plastic bags, and for each variety I take ten grape berries from the top, middle, and bottom of the clusters from fifteen different vines. Once back home, I squeeze out the juice, and then do my testing and tasting.

be, which has led to a new problem for the winemaker: too much sugar fermenting into too much alcohol.

Alcohol content for most white wine runs around 11 percent to 13 percent and 12 percent to 14 percent (with many exceptions) for reds. Red grapes are traditionally picked at a higher sugar content, because red wines rely on a higher alcohol level to give the wine more weight and body, whereas whites should be lighter and more refreshing on the palate.

Over the past five to ten years, many commercially produced wines with more than 14 percent alcohol have appeared. The power of the alcohol in these wines can overwhelm the wine's other components. Tasters refer to this imbalance as "hot." On first sip, these wines are appealing, but they soon become heavy and difficult to drink, especially with a meal.

Brix levels in grapes and juice can range from 16° to 30°, but a more typical range is from 20° to 24°. With a little math, we can determine what the resulting alcohol of the wine will be. Most yeasts will convert sugar to alcohol at a rate of between 57 percent and 61 percent; that is, for every one degree Brix, the yeast produces about 0.6 percent alcohol. So, if your grapes are picked at 20° Brix, the wine's alcohol content will be in the 11.4 percent to 12.2 percent range (20 x 57% = 11.4%). I'll discuss the factors that might determine this range in chapter nine.

### ⬤⬤ Measuring Brix

You can measure the sugar content of juice in two ways. The easiest is by using a refractometer. This instrument uses natural light to reflect a drop or two or juice on a scale quickly and easily. It can be carried out into the vineyard and requires only a few drops of juice from a berry. The downside is that refractometers are expensive, costing more than U.S. $100.

A much less expensive option is a hydrometer, which floats in a sample of juice. Special hydrometers called sacchrometers are widely available at winemaking shops. Their scale and calibration is marked by degrees Brix. The disadvantage with these, however, is that to have enough liquid in which to float the instrument, you need at least 6 or 7 ounces (200 ml) of juice, which requires quite a few grapes each time you run a Brix test.

## Hands-on Projects

To make training your palate more enjoyable, I will be assigning "homework" throughout the book. These assignments are designed to help you develop the organoleptic senses that many of us do not fully use.

# *homework*
## ASSIGNMENT

### A Taste of Fruit

**TO LEARN MORE:** Wine is made from fruit. We all have had experiences in tasting really bad and really wonderful fruit. Now take the opportunity to work on your palate by tasting, side by side, a ripe and unripe example of each. (You'll obviously have to do this when the fruit is in season.) Good examples to use are peaches, strawberries, and tomatoes. Supermarkets are always a reliable source for the underripe examples. Your own garden or a farmer's market is a source for the ripe examples. When you do your comparative tasting, pay attention to sweetness, acidity (tart or sour flavors), and, finally, flavor intensity and ripeness.

No piece of lab equipment can replace the human ability to evaluate wine aroma and flavor.

## Acidity

Wine is strongly acidic. In fact, a wine's acidity and alcohol content are its most important preservatives. More important for the winemaker, acidity contributes to the refreshing brightness of wines, especially on the wine's finish. Wines high in acidity are referred to as crisp, bracing, or tart. Wines deficient in acid are called flabby or dull. White wines depend on acidity to give them structure and longevity, whereas in red wines, acidity plays more of a supporting role to the tannins, which give the wine most of its structure.

Grapes contain two major types of acid: tartaric and malic. Together, these acids contribute to what winemakers refer to as TA—total acid, or titratable acid. Unripe grapes are piercingly acidic, but as they ripen, their sugar content increases, and the TA lowers. Warm temperatures during ripening also reduce TA (often too quickly, in the case of white wines), whereas cool temperatures keep TA higher longer. Rainfall at harvest time, too, will dilute and reduce acidity, as it does with sugar levels.

TA is expressed as the number of grams of acid in one liter of juice or wine. Usual ranges are from 5 to 9 grams/liter, on the higher side for whites, and on the lower side for reds. TA is measured by a lab test called titration. Winemaking supply houses sell acid-testing kits at a reasonable cost. These kits have all the reagents, glassware, and instructions you need to get started.

## pH

Whereas TA refers to the amount of acid in grapes, juice, or wine, pH refers to the strength of the acidity. Giving a numerical indication of the ripening process can be useful. As grapes ripen and become less acidic, the pH number rises. When we sample the grapes early in the season, pH levels are usually below 3.0. Levels for ripe grapes generally range from 3.1 to 3.6. Whites will be on the lower side (3.1 to 3.4), and reds on the higher side (3.3 to 3.6).

You'll need a pH meter to measure pH. This presents a problem for the home winemaker, because pH meters are expensive (starting at several hundred dollars [U.S.]). Unless you have access to one through work or friends, I cannot see the justification in purchasing one. Instead, I would focus on the taste, smell, and visual indicators of ripeness described in the next section.

## Aromas and Flavors

Science, lab analysis, and numbers can be useful tools in winemaking, but, ultimately, decisions must be based on the taste and perceptions of the human behind the wine. The world's best wines are all made by taste. From picking decisions to final blending decisions, taste is the primary winemaking tool. The philosophy behind this book is to help train your palate—those wonderful senses of smell and taste—to make your winemaking decisions, from when to pick and how long to ferment to when to rack.

"*I have never eaten an underripe apple, peach, apricot, pear, or fig that was enjoyable, so why would anyone think that making wine from underripe grapes produces fine wine?*"

—Robert Parker, wine critic/*The Wine Advocate*

**Aromas** Pour some of the juice from the grapes you sampled into a wineglass. Swirl the juice in the glass so that the aromas become more pronounced. Concentrate and sniff, then write down descriptors of what you smell. This first step in evaluating grape ripeness is important. When grapes are underripe, they have herbaceous qualities. When they are ripe, they tend to smell fruity. Unfortunately, unlike wine, juice alone does not have intense aromas. The alcohol in wine helps volatilize aromas, so you have to work harder with juice.

**Flavors** Now taste the juice sample. Try to focus on the acidity or tartness of the juice. This task can be difficult, because the sugar will mask the acidity. The malic acid in underripe grape juice will make it taste bitingly sour, like a green apple (malic acid is the principal acid in apples). With ripening, the acidity will soften as the acids diminish.

**Tannins** Tannins, which are found in the stems, seeds, and skins of grapes, contribute texture and structure to the finished wine. Because red wines ferment in contact with skins, seeds, and sometimes stems, tannin ripeness is a major concern for makers of red wine. We will look at how to evaluate tannin maturity in chapter eleven: Making Red Wine.

## *Balance*

Wines have myriad personalities and styles, but all good wines need to have balance. Balance refers primarily to the texture, weight, and structure of the wine. A wine is said to be balanced when all its parts alcohol, acid, and, with red wines, tannins harmonize and work together.

When tasted, alcohol has a sweet sensation. It should be in balance with the wine's acidity (the way sweetness and acidity balance in lemonade). Tannins in red wines can be drying and astringent, as they are in strong coffee or tea. They also need to be balanced by the sweetness of alcohol (as they are when you add sugar or milk to coffee).

# Aroma Wheel

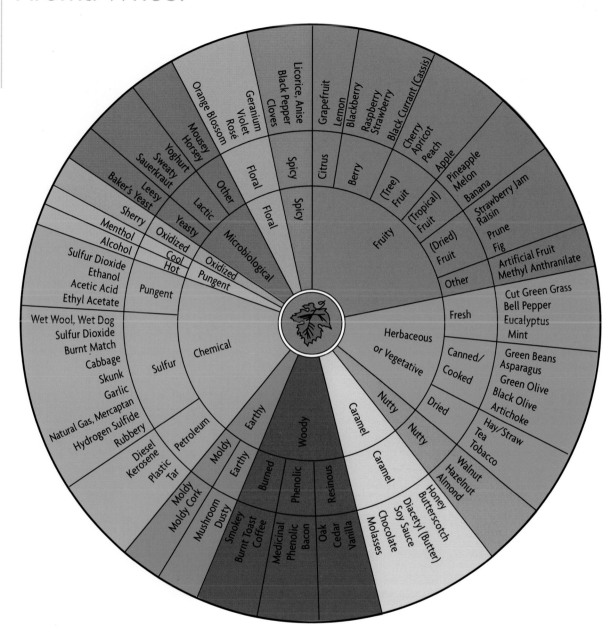

THIS AROMA WHEEL WAS DEVELOPED BY ANN NOBLE at University of California Davis, in collaboration with people in the wine industry (©1990 A C Noble) for winemakers to improve both sense of smell and vocabulary. Although it is most useful for wine, it is also invaluable for the often more difficult task of evaluating juice sample aromas. To obtain your own Aroma Wheel, see Resources, page 167.

# The Basics

## CHAPTER NINE

This chapter will address basic wine-making concepts that are applicable to both white and red wine-making. You'll need to understand some of these basic steps before moving on to the following chapters on the techniques and flow of winemaking.

Although I consider winemaking to be more of an art than a science, there are some fundamental concepts concerning sugar, acid, oxygen, and sulfur dioxide that any winemaker needs to be familiar with. Once you are comfortable with these concepts, experience will enable you to make decisions that will give your wines their own personality. Even great artists and musicians must first study and practice to master the basics before they can find their own voice. Winemakers are no different.

*There are no recipes in fine winemaking. All good winemakers change their techniques according to the season and the grapes.*

## Assessing the Must

Once the grapes are harvested, they're either pressed or crushed, depending on whether you're making white wine or red. The resulting must will soon ferment. Before it does, you need to take a small sample (a few ounces [100 ml]) and assess it by measuring the sugar (Brix) and acid (TA) levels.

In a perfect world, all grapes are harvested with balanced sugar and acid levels. In many grape growing areas of the world, this is, in fact, the case—sugar or acid adjustments are not needed. This is the goal of any wine grower: to harvest grapes at sugar and acid levels that are naturally in balance. But because this is not a perfect world, your must may need adjustments, and you will need to know how to fix any imbalances.

Be sure to take the sample before fermentation begins or the lab readings will be incorrect. Once fermentation starts, the Brix decreases as it becomes alcohol, and the acidity readings will be inaccurate (if need be, you can hold the samples under refrigeration for several days). If the sugar levels are too low or if the acidity needs to be raised, you should make additions before fermentation is finished.

### ●● Adjusting Brix

Sugar ferments to alcohol. The higher the sugar level, the higher the alcohol content. (See Desirable Harvest Brix and Alcohol Levels for Selected Wine Styles, opposite) The only exception to this rule is with sweet wines, which will be discussed in chapter ten.

If the natural sugar in the must is too low, you will want to add sugar. (Regular, store-bought cane sugar is fine.) Opinions vary as to the best timing of a sugar addition, but it absolutely needs to be done before fermentation is complete. If not, the sugar may not be fermented into alcohol, leaving you with a sweet wine.

To raise 1 gallon of must by 1° Brix, you need to add 0.084 lb. of sugar.

As an example, if you have 8 gallons of Chardonnay at 20° Brix, and you want to raise it to 22° Brix, you'll need to add 1.3 lb. of sugar.

8 (gallons) x 2 (°Brix) x 0.084 (lb) = 1.3 lb. sugar

To raise 1 liter of must by 1° Brix, you need to add 10 grams of sugar.

As an example, if you have 30 liters of Chardonnay at 20° Brix, and you want to raise it to 22° Brix, you'll need to add 600 grams of sugar.

30 (liters) x 2 (°Brix) x 10 (g) = 600 g sugar.

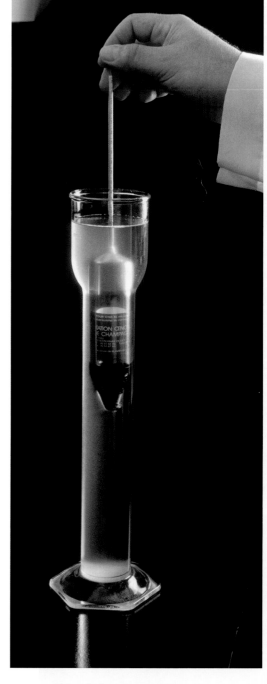

Using a hydrometer to measure Brix requires floating it in a sample of juice.

# Desirable Harvest Brix and Alcohol Levels for Selected Wine Styles

Alcohol contributes body and weight to a wine. Wines with higher alcohol levels (above 13 percent) need to have lots of flavor and concentration to balance the alcohol. Lighter wines should have a lower alcohol content and more delicate flavors. It is important to note that, generally, with white-wine fermentation, the yeast is more efficient in converting sugar to alcohol. This efficiency is because the warmer temperatures of red-wine fermentation cause some of the alcohol to evaporate.

| Wine Styles | Sugar (° Brix) | Alcohol % |
|---|---|---|
| *Light, refreshing, crisp white wines (Loire, Seyval, and Pinot Grigio)* | 19° to 21° Brix | 11 to 12.5% |
| *Full-bodied, rich white wines (Chardonnay, Rhone-style whites)* | 21° to 24° Brix | 12.5 to 14% |
| *Everyday red wines (European table wines)* | 21° to 24° Brix | 12.5 to 14% |
| *Full-bodied, age-worthy reds (Cabernet Sauvignon, Syrah, and Zinfandel)* | 23° to 25° Brix | 13 to 14% |

## ● ● Adjusting Acidity (TA)

Acid levels can vary considerably in finished wines, depending on their style. Most reds are balanced in a range of 5 to 6 grams per liter. Whites taste better when their acidity is a little higher, about 7 to 8 grams per liter, whereas the acidity levels in sweet wines can exceed 8 grams per liter. (Remember, these numbers are just guidelines.)

The acidity in your must can be greatly affected by where you live. In warmer areas, low-acid musts can be a problem, whereas in cooler regions, musts can have the opposite problem: excessive acidity. If the acidity is extremely low, add tartaric acid before or during fermentation, because the added acid tends to better integrate with the wine at this time. To increase the acidity by 1 gram per liter, add 1 gram of tartaric acid to 1 liter of wine (or 3.8 grams of tartaric acid per gallon).

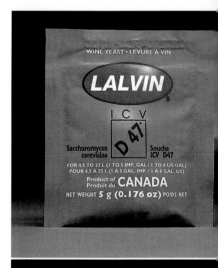

# *Chaptalization*

Adding sugar to must to increase the potential alcohol is called *chaptalization*, for Jean-Antoine Chaptal, the French chemist who discovered that sugar could be added to raise the natural Brix in juice. This method is quite common throughout the winemaking world, especially in Europe. Even Premier Cru Burgundies and classified-growth Bordeaux, considered the best wines of their regions, sometimes need a sugar boost, especially in cool, wet years.

In warm, sunny, dry regions such as California, where the sun provides abundant photosynthesis and there is little rain to dilute the grapes, the must can contain too much sugar, which can lead to excessively alcoholic wines or troubles with fermentation. Over the past several years, some California winemakers have resorted to diluting their musts with water to lower the sugar content.

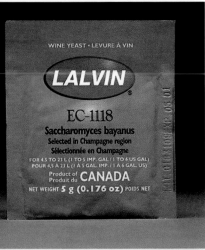

Dozens of yeast strains are available from wine supply shops. Choosing the best ones for your needs can be confusing. Because most home winemakers may not have adequate cooling or heating capability during the critical fermentation period, the most important attribute to look for is the strain's rate of fermentation. Both temperature and yeast strain will determine fermentation rate. Typically, you want a slower rate for white wines and a faster rate for reds.

To decrease acidity in high-acid musts, plan to put the wine through malolactic fermentation. New yeasts with the ability to reduce acidity are also an option. Another method of reducing acid is adding calcium carbonate, but this kind of intervention results in a wine with an unpleasant, chalky, dusty flavor and should be avoided.

Err on the side of caution when it comes to adding or reducing acid. Added acid can often make wines taste sour and hard.

## Alcoholic Fermentation

Grape juice wants to become wine. It will happen quickly on its own, without any human intervention. Our job is to control the process to some degree, to retain certain desirable flavors.

Alcoholic fermentation can be defined as yeasts converting sugar to alcohol, with carbon dioxide ($CO_2$) as a by-product. That's the simple definition. However, thousands of other conversions, which add to the flavor profile and complexities of wine, are also taking place. For example, complex compounds such as esters and aldehydes develop during fermentation and contribute to the wine wonderful aromas and flavors not found in juice. We can influence these aspects to some degree through yeast selection and temperature control.

### ●● Adding Yeast

You'll find that there are two very passionate schools when it comes to yeast: native and cultured. Native yeasts are wild or naturally occurring strains that are already present on your grapes or in your cellar (and, therefore, in your must). Cultured yeasts are specific strains that have been isolated, multiplied, packaged, and then added to the must by the winemaker.

Uninoculated fermentations (those from native yeasts) can give wines more complexity and depth, but they can also get the winemaker into trouble with high acetic acids, spoilage organisms, and stuck fermentations. Although purists feel that there is a loss of the all-important terroir by using cultured yeasts, if you are just starting out, it may be prudent to use them. With the use of cultured yeast, fermentations are faster and more predictable.

Cultured yeasts are sold in either 5-gram (0.176-oz) packs or 500-gram tins. The sales literature will state the yeast's attributes, such as its ability to give a wine more fruitiness, texture, or aroma. Personally, I think the yeast's most important characteristic is its rate of fermentation—whether a yeast is a slow or fast fermenter—because controlling the rate of fermentation determines much of the wine's style. I will make some general recommendations in subsequent chapters.

When adding yeast to the must, follow the manufacturer's instructions. Typically, the amount to add is 1 gram per gallon (1 g/4 l) of must. Rehydrate the yeast by soaking it in warm (100°F [38°C]) water for twenty minutes, and then add it to the must. You will see or smell fermentation activity in one to three days, depending on the temperature of the must (the warmer the must, the faster the yeast ferments). A light foam will develop on the surface of the must, bubbling occurs in the fermentation lock, and you will notice a yeasty, pungent aroma, especially when you put your nose to the fermentation lock.

Native yeast fermentations are also referred to as spontaneous, wild, natural, uninoculated, or indigenous. All this really means is that you don't add any yeast to the must. Studies have shown that most native yeasts are present in the wine cellars rather than on the grapes. Although there is a certain romance about doing native yeast fermentations, they can be risky. Many different yeast strains can be involved when allowing uninoculated fermentations, and some of the strains can produce unpleasant aromas. Then again, most of the best wines in the world are produced by native yeasts. The problem is that you never know what is going to happen until you try it. If you are a novice winemaker, you should proceed with caution. Native yeast fermentations are slower and more susceptible to problems such as stuck fermentations and hydrogen sulfide production than inoculated fermentations. Using cultured yeast, at least initially, may be the safer choice, until you gain experience.

Once fermentation has begun, you may want to add yeast food, also known as yeast nutrients, to the must. Several brands of nutrients are available. All have nitrogen, the food source most commonly lacking in grapes. Most also contain other vitamins and minerals the yeast needs to continue fermentation to the finish (when all the sugar has been

*Grape juice wants to become wine. It will happen quickly on its own, without any human intervention. Our job is to control the process to some degree . . . .*

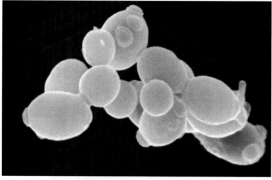

**Yeast cells, close up. You don't make wine—these guys do all the work.**

converted into alcohol). Typically, nutrients are added at a rate of 1 to 2 grams per gallon (0.25 to 0.5 grams per liter) of must.

Adding nutrients helps to prevent two major problems with fermentation caused by a lack of sufficient yeast food. The first is stuck fermentation. A fermentation gets stuck when it seems to be going quite well, then, toward the finish, simply stops prematurely, leaving a wine with undesirable sweetness. It is extremely difficult to restart fermentation. Nutrient deficiency can also lead to the production of undesirable hydrogen sulfide ($H_2S$) aromas, caused when the yeast becomes stressed from lack of nutrients. These sulfide aromas smell like rotten eggs. $H_2S$ is the compound added to natural and propane gases so that leaks are easily identified—the pungent, unpleasant odor is unmistakable and not a good thing to have in your wine.

## Fermenting Temperature

The temperature of the fermenting wine has a significant influence on the wine's style, aromas, flavors, and rate of fermentation. Yeast ferments the fastest at temperatures ranging from 75°F to 90°F (24°C to 32°C). Cooler temperatures slow yeast activity. Very hot temperatures (above 95°F [35°C]) can actually kill the yeast. Using a thermometer, measure the temperature of the fermenting wine once a day. Whites should ferment slowly—slow, cool fermentations preserve fruitiness—and reds quickly—quick, warm fermentations extract more flavor and color from the skins.

To achieve a fresh, fruity style white, ferment the must at a temperature between 45°F and 60°F (7°C to 15°C). Within this temperature range, it should take three to six weeks for fermentation to finish. Full-bodied, richer-style whites, fermenting at a temperature of between 55°F and 75°F (13°C to 14°C), will take one to three weeks to complete. Reds generally ferment at a warmer temperature, 75°F to 90°F (24°C to 32°C), which results in a short fermentation time of five to ten days.

# Malolactic Fermentation

Malolactic fermentation (MLF), also referred to as secondary fermentation, does not involve yeast, sugar, or alcohol. It is a bacterial fermentation, which changes the grape's natural, sour-tasting malic acid into smoother lactic acid. Not all wines undergo MLF; all reds do, but only some white wines do.

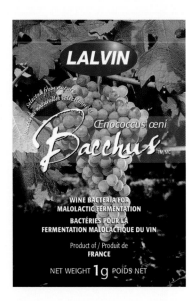

Malolactic bacteria, like wine yeasts, occur naturally, but cultured bacteria can also be purchased.

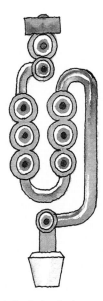

Fermentation locks, also known as air locks, come in many different styles (one of the more common types is shown above), but all serve the same purpose: They allow $CO_2$ gas from fermentation to escape and prevent fruit flies and air from entering.

## *Chardonnay*

Grown throughout the world's grape growing regions, Chardonnay produces wines that have often been fermented or aged in oak barrels, to give the wine vanilla flavors, or put through malolactic fermentation, to give the wine a rich, buttery taste. Most white Burgundy is made from the Chardonnay grape.

**Taste characteristics:** New World—pear, apple, or tropical fruit, full-bodied, often with vanilla and toasty oak influence. Burgundy—mineral, hazelnut, yeasty

**Serve:** chilled, at about 45°F to 50°F (7°C to 10°C)

**Pair with:** chicken and dishes made with butter or a cream sauce

Malic acid has a strong impact on the palate. Its bracing acidity is not harmonious with the tannins in red wine. Nor is it complementary to some round, full-style white wines. It can, however, be pleasantly refreshing in young, crisp, fruity white wines.

Lactic acid, a dairy acid found in butter, milk, and cheese, does not have the same level of tartness as malic acid. In MLF, malolactic bacteria added to the wine consume the malic acid and convert it to lactic acid and carbon dioxide, ultimately reducing the wine's TA. MLF also lessens the palate's perception of the strength of the wine's acidity, because lactic acid is not as strong as malic acid. MLF can also change the flavor, aroma, and mouth-feel (texture) of wine—it loses its fresh, green-apple character and

## *tip*

As a rule of thumb, try to minimize racking white wines and maximize racking young red wines. White wines lose their freshness quickly when they are exposed to the air during racking. Young red wines, on the other hand, will often become more supple and refined when small amounts of air are introduced during the early aging process.

*tip*

•••• 
•••
••

**Always think twice
before you add anything to
juice or wine. The carpenters'
adage, "measure twice, cut
once," is just as true for
winemakers. Once you make
an addition, you can't remove it.
A miscalculation or mix-up can
ruin a batch of wine.**

develops a rich, buttery quality. Chardonnays are a good example of the kinds of wine that undergo MLF. Chardonnays that have not undergone MLF have a noticeable green-apple aroma and crisp flavor profile. Those that have undergone MLF lean more to the buttery side. To gain more complexity, some winemakers put some, but not all, of their Chardonnay wine through MLF, and then blend the two batches before bottling.

Wine stability is a major concern for home winemakers. The bacteria that ferment malic acid can be naturally present in the wine. When a wine contains malic acid, it is vulnerable to MLF, whether the winemaker desires it or not. This is just as true of wines that have been bottled. Bottled wines that have not undergone MLF are at risk for MLF occurring in the bottle, the result being a fizzy ($CO_2$ is a by-product), cloudy, and probably off-tasting wine. Although commercial wineries avoid this problem by filtering these wines, this type of filtration (see chapter seven), though possible, is very expensive for the home winemaker. If you don't have a filter, I advise putting all your wines through MLF. During or just after alcoholic fermentation are the best times for MLF to occur—this is when conditions for the ML bacteria to do their job are ideal.

## *Racking*

To rack juice or wine from one vessel to another, set the carboy from which you are racking (the one with the liquid in it) on a table or bench, so it is higher than the empty carboy—the higher the level, the faster the flow. Place one end of a siphon tube about halfway into the wine, and then slowly but consistently suck the end of the tube until the wine flows up the tube and over the lip of the carboy. Quickly place the end of the tube in the bottom of the empty carboy—you want to reduce splashing and avoid air pickup (if not desired). Once the flow is constant, slide the other end of the tube to the bottom of the higher carboy, making sure not to suck up too much lees.

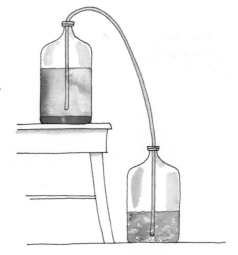

### ●● To Inoculate or Not to Inoculate

Malolactic fermentations, just as with alcoholic fermentations, can either be inoculated with an ML culture or left uninoculated. ML bacteria prefer warm temperatures (above 68°F [20°C]), low alcohol content, lots of nutrients, and low $SO_2$ (sulfur dioxide) levels. These conditions are well met during and just after alcoholic fermentation. ML bacteria can interfere with alcoholic fermentation; inoculating after alcoholic fermentation is complete lowers the risk of a stuck alcoholic fermentation. As with yeast, if you inoculate with a cultured ML bacteria, follow the instructions on the package. Typically, the powdered bacteria are rehydrated in warm water and then mixed with the wine just after alcoholic fermentation is complete. MLF will produce a very small amount of $CO_2$, which will occasionally bubble the water in the fermentation lock. Usually it takes a few weeks to complete. At this point, we move on to the next technique: racking.

# *homework*
### ASSIGNMENT

## Wine Style and Oxygen

**TO LEARN MORE:** Some wines are made in a way that excludes oxygen as much as possible, a process called reductive wine-making. Other wines are purposely exposed to oxygen. These are oxidized wines. Both are intentional wine styles and are not considered flaws.

Train your palate by purchasing examples of each style. Examples of reductive-style wines are all whites. They include wines made from the Sauvignon Blanc grape and include Sancerre and Pouilly-Fumés, as well as German Rieslings and some young Chablis. Reductive aromas will be fresh and pungent, with herbal, mineral, fruity aromas. Oxidative-style examples include sherry, madeira, Baynuls, and amarone. These are all powerful wines, with a roasted, nutty, cooked character.

## Racking

Racking is the winemaking term for transferring juice or wine from one container to another. Home winemakers generally perform this task with a siphon tube. Racking is done to remove the relatively clear juice or wine from the sediment and to introduce oxygen into the juice or wine. (I discuss the reasons for making different racking decisions throughout the book.)

Although it is a beneficial step in the process, racking can be done too often (a common mistake made by many new winemakers). Racking is oxidative, meaning the wine absorbs oxygen, and racking too often can tire out the wine by exposing it to too much oxygen.

## The Role of Oxygen

Oxygen can be your best friend or your worst enemy. In this section, I offer some guidelines for using air (oxygen) to your advantage and, even more important, for protecting your wine from oxygen when exposure is undesirable. Because oxygen is in the air, I'll use the terms air and oxygen interchangeably.

### ● ●  When Air Is Desirable

- ● Yeast cells need oxygen to multiply and thrive. One reason fermentations run into problems, especially with dreaded sulfide aromas, is that the yeast cells are starving for oxygen. Therefore, some winemakers will aerate, or oxygenate, the must or fermenting wine by introducing oxygen into it. This process can be done by "splash racking": when siphoning, the end of the siphon hose is inserted only slightly into the mouth of the receiving carboy, allowing the wine or juice to splash as it falls to the bottom of the carboy, thus picking up oxygen. Over time, you will learn that some wines and styles (such as reds and Chardonnays) benefit greatly from splash racking, whereas others (aromatic whites such as Sauvignon Blanc and Riesling) lose freshness if splash racking is overdone.

- ● Hydrogen sulfide and sulfide-aroma problems can be fixed, if the problem is caught early enough, by aerating a wine. It's important to smell your wines during and just after fermentation.

*Siphoning* takes a bit of practice. Start by setting one carboy on a bench or table, so it is higher than the other— you'll have gravity on your side.

If you detect the characteristic rotten-egg aroma, immediate splash racking usually dissipates it. But if you don't act quickly, the $H_2S$ evolves into compounds known as mercaptans, which are reminiscent of skunk and garlic odors. Mercaptans do not disappear with aeration.

- Regular introduction of air will soften and integrate the tannins of fermenting and young (six months or younger) red wines and contribute to a more supple and harmonious mouth-feel and finish. Some red winemaking techniques include daily aerations during fermentation and rackings every thirty to sixty days immediately after fermentation, to soften highly tannic wines such as Cabernet Sauvignon, Petit Verdot, or Tannat.

## When Air Is Not Desirable

If wines are exposed to too much oxygen, they oxidize. When you bite into an apple, then set it down for an hour or so, the exposed area begins to brown. This is oxidation. Juice and wine do the same thing—the wine turns brown and takes on a cooked, caramelized flavor. Although this may be desirable with a few wines (sherry, madeira, and Vin Santo, for example), in most cases, wines with this characteristic are considered flawed or spoiled. The dreaded Acetobacter bacteria, which turns wine to vinegar, also needs oxygen to grow.

The following tips prevent too much oxygen ($O_2$) pickup:

- Rack infrequently and keep wine cool. Young wines are much more resistant to oxidation than older wines. During and just after fermentation, wines are saturated with carbon dioxide, a by-product of fermentation. The $CO_2$ acts as a buffer against $O_2$ pickup. Racking stirs up the new wine and causes it to release lots of $CO_2$ (just like shaking a can of beer before opening it). Warmer temperatures also will cause $CO_2$ to dissipate quickly. Wine aged in oak barrels (which are porous, allowing the $CO_2$ to escape slowly), racked frequently, and aged in warm cellars quickly loses the protection of $CO_2$. After the first winter of a wine's life, most of the $CO_2$ dissipates.

*tip*

You may want to practice siphoning with water before you work with juice or wine. Water is less expensive and easier to clean up when you make mistakes!

- Avoid leaving headspace (known as ullage) in a container when aging wine. During fermentation, yeast produces so much $CO_2$ that any headspace is filled with inert $CO_2$ rather than $O_2$. However, once the wine is racked after fermentation, any remaining headspace will contain some $O_2$, which will slowly be absorbed by the wine. You will eventually see a film of bacteria or yeast growth on the surface of a wine aging in a partially filled container. Always age wine in a full container. Therefore, you should always have varying sizes of bottles and carboys on hand.

- Inert gases, such as carbon dioxide and nitrogen, are effective in reducing oxygen pickup during racking and bottling. By filling an empty carboy, barrel, or bottle with the gas before the wine enters, the wine will pick up the neutral gas instead of absorbing oxygen. Useful for wine drinkers as well as wine-makers, these wine-preserving gases help to slow oxidation that occurs when a bottle of wine is not fully consumed and left overnight with a headspace. These gases are available from wine shops in small, easy-to-use dispensers.

Two other contributors to reducing oxygen pickup are lees and sulfur dioxide (see more on these next). Fine lees are the spent yeast cells that add flavor and texture to an aging wine. They are also great oxygen scavengers and can help protect a wine from excessive oxygen pickup.

Sulfur dioxide can also help protect wine from oxygen. As we will learn, the more $SO_2$ added to a wine, the more protected it will be.

Managing air contact with wine can be difficult for new winemakers. I will discuss techniques in greater detail in the white and red winemaking chapters. The best word of advice is that if you are unsure, err on the side of reducing $O_2$ pickup. More wines are spoiled because of excessive air contact than by not enough.

Your lab can be as simple or as elaborate as you like. Novice winemakers, however, will need only a table in the corner of the kitchen or garage to perform wine tests.

# The Role of Sulfur Dioxide

Sulfur-dioxide, $SO_2$, and sulfur are, in wine-maker-speak, interchangeable terms. They refer to the one additive that is used almost universally in winemaking and has been for centuries. $SO_2$ is an important winemaking tool for two reasons—it can help protect wines against both oxidation and unwanted microbial spoilage.

### ●● $SO_2$ as an Antioxidant

$SO_2$'s antioxidant characteristic is the most important reason that it is used in wine-making. When exposed to air, juice and wine will absorb oxygen, and, as you now know, we need to control the timing and amount of $O_2$ absorbed. $SO_2$, when added to wine, binds up much of the oxygen before the oxygen can react with the wine's components.

### ●● $SO_2$ as an Antimicrobial

$SO_2$ can slow the growth of undesirable yeasts and bacteria. Although $SO_2$ levels in winemaking will not kill yeasts and bacteria or indefinitely protect a juice or wine from spoilage problems, it can help in certain situations, such as at crush, when the grapes have rot and undesirable yeasts. $SO_2$ additions slow the growth of these yeasts and allow $SO_2$-resistant, cultured yeasts to take over fermentation.

### ●● Adding $SO_2$

The most common times to add $SO_2$ to juice or wine follow:

- **To the must**  Adding a small amount (20 to 40 parts per million [ppm]) of $SO_2$ to white juice or crushed red grapes binds up some oxygen for the later use of the fermenting yeast

## Sulfites and Health Issues, Real and Imagined

I intend to address sulfites only as they relate to making fine wine. However, I am regularly asked by customers about the health impact of sulfites in wine. I reply that I am a winemaker, not a physician. A very small segment of the population, mostly people with asthma, are sensitive to sulfites and should probably avoid drinking wine. Wines sold in the United States are now labeled "Contains Sulfites," unless they contain sulfite levels less than 10 ppm. Most red wines contain significantly fewer sulfites than white wines.

In recent decades, research and experience have taught us how to better manage the use of $O_2$ and, in turn, reduce $SO_2$ amounts. Today's wines have many fewer sulfites than they have had historically, principally because we understand how other methods, such as the use of inert gases and lees, can help achieve the same goal. However, even though we have reduced its use, $SO_2$ is still considered necessary in winemaking.

*tip*

Because the amount of potassium metabisulfite added to wine is so small, it is difficult to measure accurately. Some home winemakers make up a 1 percent or 10 percent solution of metabisulfite and water and then add this solution to their wines.

and slows the activity of undesirable spoilage bacteria or yeast. Increase the amount of $SO_2$ if there are rot problems with the grapes.

- **Postfermentation**   After all alcoholic and malolactic fermentation is complete, $SO_2$ is added to slow oxygen pickup and hinder the development of undesirable organisms such as Brettanomyces, a spoilage yeast, and Acetobacter, the vinegar bacteria that needs oxygen to survive. Use larger amounts of $SO_2$ for wines that will not undergo MLF.

- **During aging**   As $SO_2$ bonds with oxygen, the amount of available oxygen is reduced. The style of wine and the amount of racking you do will determine how much $SO_2$ you need to add during aging.

- **At bottling**   Bottling introduces a fair amount of $SO_2$ to the wine. $SO_2$ levels should be high enough to bind up some of the $O_2$ and protect the wine.

# Adding $SO_2$

Below is a conversion table for measuring amounts of $SO_2$.

1 Campden tablet = 0.55 grams

$1/4$ (level) teaspoon = 1.6 grams

One ppm of $SO_2$ to one gallon of juice or wine = 0.0064 grams. With this information, you can calculate how much $SO_2$ to add. For example, if you need to add 30 ppm, and you have a volume of 6 gallons, then:

30 (ppm) x 6 (gallons) x 0.0064 = 1.152 grams of potassium metabisulfite.

On a metric scale, the calculation is: 1 ppm to 1 liter of juice or wine = 0.0017 grams. For example, if you need to add 50 ppm to 60 liters, then:

50 (ppm) x 60 (liters) x 0.0017 = 5.1grams of potassium metabisulfite

Check and double-check your math, especially the decimal points! Adding too much $SO_2$ can make your wine undrinkable.

## ●● Free SO₂

Because SO₂ becomes less effective over time, we have to add additional amounts of sulfites to aging wines. The part of an SO₂ addition that remains effective (the part that does not bind with oxygen) is called free SO₂. Typically, about half of the $SO_2$ added will bind up immediately, leaving the other half as free SO₂. Over subsequent months, more and more of the free SO₂ will bind. Therefore, we need to measure the amount of free SO₂ in a wine before we decide to make another addition.

## ●● Adding SO₂

Although SO₂ levels are measured in parts per million (ppm), it is added in a powdered form (potassium metabisulfite) that is measured by weight (grams). The amounts added on a small scale are miniscule. Because you will probably not have a scale capable of measuring grams or fractions of grams, I have provided a conversion table that measures by quarter-teaspoons and by Campden tablets, SO₂ in a compressed pill form, are available from winemaking suppliers.

Throughout the rest of this book I will make SO₂ addition recommendations for given wines and winemaking styles. To help understand the timing and general amounts to add, the chart on page 105 may be useful.

## ●● Measuring SO₂

During wine aging, it is a good idea to measure the amount of free SO₂ actually in the wine before deciding how much more, if any, to add. Naturally, the most accurate methods to measure SO₂ levels are quite involved and expensive. However, I can recommend using a simple test kit manufactured by Chemetrics to measure free SO₂. It uses the principal of a test called the Ripper method but requires nothing more from you than the ability to observe a color change. The test kit is simple, inexpensive, and widely available at winemaking supply houses.

# Lees

Lees is the sediment that forms over time on the bottom of a vessel holding juice or wine. Juice and wine contain solids that make them cloudy when they are young. With time, these solids drop to the bottom of the container and form lees. Lees come in several types. In some cases, they can be desirable, and at other times, undesirable. A brief review of the different types of lees follows. In later chapters, I will discuss their importance to specific wine styles.

Carboys filled with fermenting white and red wines are fitted with fermentation locks to allow $CO_2$ to escape. Note the fine lees in the bottom of the carboy in the foreground.

# Timing of SO₂ Additions

| To Must (red or white juice | Type of Wine | Postfermentation (alcoholic and malolactic) | Range of Desired Free SO₂ Levels during Aging |
|---|---|---|---|
| Add 20–50 ppm (up to 100 ppm if there is rot in the juice) | ➤ *Fresh, aromatic whites:* | 60–100 ppm | 30–50 ppm |
| | ➤ *Full-bodied lees and barrel-aged whites:* | 40–60 ppm | 20–30 ppm |
| | ➤ *Reds:* | 20–40 ppm | 15–25 ppm |

*C*arboys filled with fermenting white and red wines are fitted with fermentation locks, to allow CO$_2$ to escape. Note the fine lees in the bottom of the carboy in the foreground.

## ●● Juice Lees

When making white wines, the freshly pressed juice is typically left for one or two days before fermentation begins to settle out some of its cloudiness. The sediment that forms during settling, called juice lees, is mostly grape solids. Most winemakers consider it undesirable. The clear juice is carefully racked off of the lees, and the lees is discarded. Some winemakers prefer to leave some cloudiness in their white juice. This is a wine style decision that I will discuss in chapter ten.

## ●● Gross Lees

A lot of lees forms immediately after fermentation. Called gross lees, it is a mixture of dead yeast cells and grape pieces. Wines are usually racked off of their gross lees very soon after fermentation, because they can contribute to hydrogen sulfide problems. However, again, there are exceptions in which a winemaker may decide to age a wine on its gross lees.

## ●● Fine Lees

Fine lees are the subsequent lees that form after racking the wine off of its gross lees. These lees are often very desirable in winemaking because they are primarily spent yeast that can contribute desirable flavors and texture to a wine. They also have antioxidant abilities—they are oxygen scavengers and help keep a wine fresh. A common technique called *batonnage* is often used to stir up these lees, so as to maximize their impact on the wine.

# Making White Wines

## CHAPTER TEN

*F*ew things in life are more pleasurable than enjoying a cool glass of crisp white wine with fresh fish on a warm summer evening. I love white wines that are light, refreshing, and bracing.

But perhaps your tastes run toward full-bodied, soft, oaky whites. Wine style preference is individual, and before you start making wine, you need to know where you are going. You should have a wine style in mind, even before picking your grapes: When you harvest your grapes has the most significant influence on the style of your white wine.

Gaining experience by tasting wines of different styles will enable you to direct winemaking decisions into the style you desire. Be sure to try out the "Homework Assignments," which are designed to help you develop your palate and your wine-style preferences.

Unless otherwise stated, in the following chapters, the wines referred to as "dry" have no discernable sweetness.

*T*he pleasure of white wines derives from their aromas and crisp, refreshing acidity. Your job is to retain these two grape components in the wine.

## When to Pick

Variety and terroir are predetermined at this stage of the game. Now it's up to the winemaker to understand how to take advantage of the strengths of the ripening grapes under ever-changing circumstances— in other words, the weather.

Hot, dry conditions produce grapes with lots of sugar and low acidity. Cool, wet conditions preserve acidity and keep sugars low. Rain during ripening can also contribute to rot. All these factors are considered when deciding when to pick the grapes, and in each vintage, these factors are different, which is why flexibility is important. With white wines, I find that flavor and aroma profiles, along with acidity, are the most important factors in determining wine style and when to pick the grapes.

The table (opposite) describes flavor development as grapes ripen. These same flavors will be in the finished wine. As the grapes ripen, their acidity (TA) falls. Most of the acidity lost is malic acid. If the grape's TA is above 9 or 10 grams per liter, the resulting wine will likely be dry and bracing, with a somewhat hard finish. Sweet wines can be quite lovely with this level of acidity, because the sugar will balance the tartness (see the section on sweet wines at the end of this chapter). In hot years, however, a white-wine grape's acidity may fall below 6 grams per liter, resulting in a flabby wine. If this is the case, you will probably have to add tartaric acid (see chapter nine).

The natural Brix level in your grapes determines the alcohol percentage in the finished wine. White-wine fermentations usually convert sugar to alcohol at a conversion rate of 0.58 to 0.61 (for every degree Brix, the yeast will produce about 0.6 percent alcohol.) For example, if the natural sugar in your grapes is 20° Brix, the resulting alcohol level will be between 11.6 to 12.2. If the natural sugar level is too low to produce the desired alcohol (for whites, usually in the 11 percent to 12.5 percent range), you will have to add sugar (see Chapter Nine).

*When harvesting your grapes, the key word to keep in mind is gentle. Much of a white wine's finesse comes from carefully handling and pressing the grapes.*

# Grape Flavor Profiles

The following table developed by Foris Vineyards Winery describes the changing flavor profiles of ripening grapes. As grapes begin to ripen, their flavors and aromas are vegetal. As time passes, more fruit evolves.

| Grape Type | Underripe | Ideal | Overripe |
|---|---|---|---|
| *Cabernet* | vegetal, green beans, green pepper, cranberry acidic, hard, lean, hollow | bramble, blackberry raspberry, bright, tea, cedar, soft, velvety | prune, cooked, dull, blueberry jam, flabby |
| *Merlot* | vegetal, green beans, dill, green pepper, choke cherry, cranberry, acidic, hard, lean | chocolate-covered cherries, tea, evergreen, mint, soft, velvety, bright | prune, cooked, canned cherry, plum jam, black fruits, alcoholic, flabby |
| *Pinot Noir* | strawberry, cranberry stemmy, herbal, acidic, hard, short | cassis, cherry, red fruits, mushroom, fleshy, balanced, bright red fruits, soft, velvety | cooked black cherry, prune, plum, black fruits, alcoholic, dull, flabby |
| *Chardonnay* | green apple, grapefruit, acidic, hard, bitter, steely | pear, floral, citrus, apple, lemon, stone fruits, melon, soft but bright | lack of distinct fruits, alcoholic, flabby |
| *Pinot Gris* | green apple, citrus, acidic, hard, short, steely | pear, melons, baked bread; soft but bright, crisp, rich | cooked fruits, overly soft and alcoholic, flabby |
| *Gewürztraminer* | citrus, floral, lack of complexity, acidic, steely, hard | grapefruit, lychee, rose, soapy, orange peel, spicy, rich, oily, complex, balanced | medicinal, floral, lack of complexity, no balance, flabby |

## Harvesting the Grapes

When harvesting your grapes, the key word to keep in mind is gentle.
Much of a white wine's finesse comes from carefully handling and pressing
the grapes. Grape skins contain bitter and astringent compounds known
as phenols. These compounds are desirable in most red wines, and red
winemaking is geared toward their extraction. In white wines, however,
phenols are not desirable, and the excessive extraction of skin compounds
can result in a coarse, bitter wine.

Phenolic compounds are released the moment a grape berry is
cracked open. Gently picking, transporting, and sorting the grapes helps
assure the quality of the wine.

Picking should be done during the coolest time of the day. Cool grapes
retain more aromas and are better protected against bitter compounds
than when the skins are broken. Warm grapes absorb more of the bitterness from the skins and also produce warm juice, which can ferment too
quickly and lose delicate fruit aromas. Handle the grapes gently, and place
them in harvest containers. Once picked, white-wine grapes should be
either pressed immediately or chilled.

## Sorting

Rain before and during harvest can cause rot, which is a big heartbreak
for the grower. Not only does rot reduce yields, it increases the time it
takes to harvest because of the need to sort out the bad fruit.

Two general types of rot occur:

- **Sour rot**   Sour rot is caused by numerous microorganisms,
  with the main culprit being Acetobacter, also known as the
  vinegar bacteria. Even a small amount of sour rot can lead to
  wines high in acetic acid (also known as volatile acidity or
  vinegar acid. The rot-affected grapes tend to have a tan,
  pinkish hue to them. I like to smell for sour rot. The pungent,
  vinegary smell is unmistakable. Even small amounts in the juice
  can reduce fruitiness and contribute to bitterness in the wine.

- **Botrytis cinerea, botrytis rot**   (also known as gray mold
  or noble rot). Some of the most magnificent sweet white
  wines in the world are made when botrytis infections are

*tip*

If you press whole
clusters of your white grapes
(no crushing), you will find that
the resulting juice is quite clear.
In this case, some winemakers
will skip the settling stage and
go right to fermentation.

# *homework*
## ASSIGNMENT

## White Wine Styles

*TO LEARN MORE:* At the risk of overgeneralizing, white wines generally fall into two distinct style categories: light, crisp, and clean; and full-bodied, rich, and complex. Crisp, clean wines are usually low in alcohol content (less than 12 percent) and high in acidity. They are great with simply prepared fish and are very refreshing, which makes them ideal for enjoying in warmer weather. They also tend to be inexpensive. Examples include the dry wines from Germany and the Loire Valley, Chablis (not premier or Grand Crus), and Pinot Grigio from Italy.

Full-bodied, rich wines tend to have more alcohol (13 percent or more) and are, sometimes, lower in acidity. I find them more enjoyable in cooler weather, with more substantial meals, such as roasted chicken or white meats. These wines are more expensive. They include White Rhônes, Premier or Grand Cru Burgundies, and California or Australian Chardonnays.

To better understand style differences, taste two wines made from the same grape side by side.

1. Compare a full-bodied Alsatian Pinot Gris to an light Italian Pinot Grigio. (Pinot Gris and Pinot Grigio refer to the same grape; one is French and the other Italian.)

2. Do the same with a Californian or Australian Chardonnay (full) and a light French Chablis. (Chablis is made from the Chardonnay grape.)

3. Do the same with a Californian Sauvignon Blanc (full) and a light Sancerre or Pouilly-Fumé (made from Sauvignon Blanc grapes).

fortuitously timed (see the Homework Assignment, page 125). Unfortunately, botrytis often infects the grapes before they are ripe, so that the flavors they concentrate are tart, green, and undesirable. Because of its distinct gray color on grape skins, botrytis rot is easily recognizable to anyone attempting to sort it out.

Sunburned grapes should also be discarded. This triage can be done either in the vineyard, as you are picking, or at the pressing area.

## Getting the Juice Out

At this point, the grapes are placed directly into the press for pressing. If you have a destemmer or crusher, you may choose to destem and lightly crush the grapes first. The advantage of crushing is more logistical than anything else. Not only can you put twice the volume of crushed grapes than whole clusters into a given press, but crushed grapes will yield more juice, because much of the juice will run freely from crushed grapes (free-run juice), even before pressure is applied by the press. Also, with crushed grapes, the individual berries do not have to be popped by the pressure of the press. With whole-cluster pressing, it is common to see some intact berries after you are finished pressing. The downside is that there is a better chance of extracting too much bitterness from the skins.

Place a tub under the crusher to catch the crushed grapes. When it is full, pour the crushed grapes into the press. You can also place the crusher on top of the press and have the crushed grapes fall directly into the press.

Once the grapes are in the press, apply pressure slowly and gently until you see juice begin to flow through the slats. If the grapes were crushed, some of the juice will have already run out and into the press's tray, so have a bucket positioned below the press tray's lip to catch the flow. Stop applying pressure and wait for a few minutes, until the flow eases, then apply a bit more pressure. After you do this two or three times, you will need to get into the grapes and stir them up with your hands to reconfigure them inside the press. Then start the pressing cycle over again.

At each "tumbling," taste the juice. After about the second or third cycle, you might find that the juice does not taste as fresh and has a some-what bitter aftertaste. This "press juice" is considered inferior because of

*tip*

You need about 12 lb. of grapes to make 1 gallon (or about 1.5 kg to make 1 liter) of juice. By the time the juice becomes finished wine, you will lose 10 percent of the volume to solids settling—and sampling. (Percentages can vary according to sampling habits and frequency!)

# Making White Wine

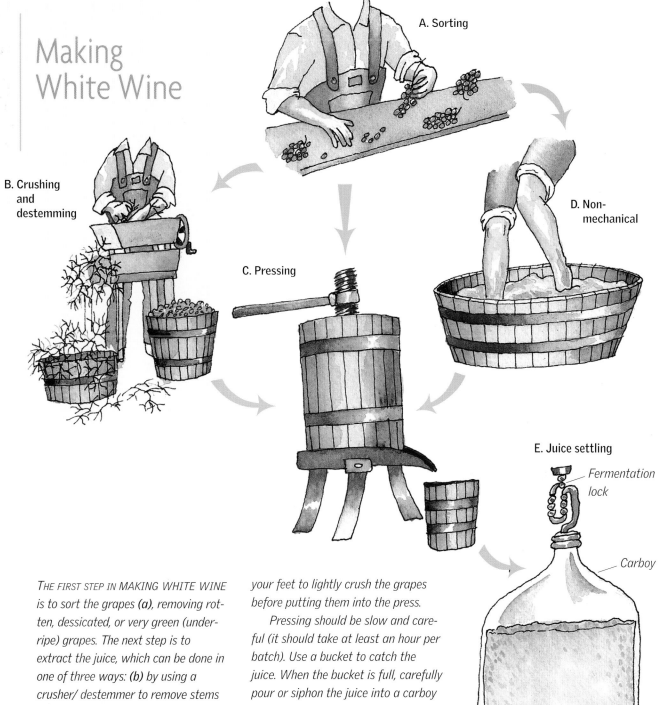

**A. Sorting**

**B. Crushing and destemming**

**C. Pressing**

**D. Non-mechanical**

**E. Juice settling**

Fermentation lock

Carboy

*THE FIRST STEP IN MAKING WHITE WINE is to sort the grapes (a), removing rotten, dessicated, or very green (underripe) grapes. The next step is to extract the juice, which can be done in one of three ways: (b) by using a crusher/ destemmer to remove stems and lightly crush the grapes, and then putting the crushed grapes into the press; (c) by placing the whole clusters directly into the press; or (d) by using your feet to lightly crush the grapes before putting them into the press.*

*Pressing should be slow and careful (it should take at least an hour per batch). Use a bucket to catch the juice. When the bucket is full, carefully pour or siphon the juice into a carboy (e). Allow the juice to settle out its solids for a day, then carefully rack the clear juice into another carboy to start fermentation.*

its bitterness and lack of fresh acidity. Keep the press juice separate from the initial "free run" juice by putting it in another carboy.

Press juice usually comprises less than 20 percent of the total juice yielded. You will want to treat it slightly differently than the free-run juice, because press juice can result in bitter wine. If the press juice is fined (see Gelatin Fining, below) for bitterness, it may be good to use for blending, but taste it first and decide if it is acceptable. Blending the press juice back into the main juice or wine could contribute bitterness to the entire lot. Its best use may be for cooking!

## Juice Treatments

You now have murky, cloudy juice in your carboy. If there is headspace in the bottle, spritz some inert gas into it to slow down surface oxidation while the juice settles overnight. Check the temperature of the juice with a floating thermometer. You want the juice to be cool (below 60°F [15°C]). If it is warmer, try to chill it (this is where an old refrigerator comes in handy) so it doesn't begin to ferment before it has a chance to settle its solids. Fermentation will keep the solids in suspension.

If your grapes were healthy, add 20 to 40 ppm $SO_2$ to the juice; add up to 80 ppm if the grapes had rot problems (see chapter nine for instructions on adding $SO_2$). Then, take a juice sample—2 to 4 ounces (60 to 120 ml)—and run sugar and TA tests, being sure to make any sugar or acid corrections before or during fermentation (see Chapter Nine). Taste the juice for bitterness, particularly with press juice. If you taste bitter elements, you may want to fine the juice with gelatin.

### ●● Gelatin Fining

Fining is the winemaking term for temporarily introducing a material (a fining agent) to juice or wine to improve its flavor, protein stability (see chapter twelve), and clarification. I'll cover many fining agents in depth in chapter twelve, but for right now, I will discuss juice fining with gelatin.

Crushing white grapes before pressing helps to release the juice.

*tip*

Buy your gelatin from a winemaking supply shop—it is a better grade than what you will find in the grocery store.

Gelatin is used in fining to reduce bitterness. It is most commonly used in press juice (not the free-run juice). The proteins in gelatin bind with the phenols in the juice and literally pull them to the bottom of the carboy. This is the principle of fining—an agent, such as gelatin, is mixed into the juice or wine and binds with a specific undesirable compound. Both fall to the bottom into the lees. The juice or wine is then racked off of its lees.

One of the problems with fining is that the agent can also strip the juice or wine of the desirable compounds that give wine flavor, structure, and body. This is why fining is sometimes done to juice instead of wine. Juice is considered a less complex, less delicate beverage than wine and can handle rougher treatment without the same detrimental effects.

**Adding the Fining Agent**    Once you have finished pressing and know the quantity of juice that needs fining, add 0.5 to 1.0 grams of fining agent per gallon (0.1 to 0.3 grams per liter), depending on the level of bitterness you perceive in the juice. Mix the powdered gelatin with a small quantity of cold water, then mix this into the juice. Let the gelatin settle for a day or two, then rack the clear juice off of its lees (see chapter nine). It is principally the press juice and certain grape varieties such as Gewürzraminer, Muscat, Seyval, and Vidal, which are known for their bitterness, that need this fining.

## Letting the Juice Settle

Juice is usually quite cloudy after pressing. In most cases, you will want to settle the juice at least overnight, if not longer. Keep the temperature of the must below 60°F (15°C), or you could run the risk of spontaneous wild-yeast fermentation starting before you rack the juice off of its lees. The cloudiness is mostly from small pieces of grape skins and pulp. These solids can contribute to hydrogen sulfide problems at the end of fermentation. Most winemakers allow at least some of these solids to settle out of the juice, but how clear you want your juice before racking it off of its juice lees is a question of style. For a delicate, fruity, clean style of wine, you want to ferment

This antique cider press was used somewhat successfully for grapes. The grapes are first "crushed" by the grinder below the hopper, and then the basket is slid into place under the hand press. The juice flows into a bucket.

fairly clear juice. For a rich, earthy, more complex white wine, you may want to ferment juice with some cloudiness. Some winemakers purposely allow some of the juice lees to be sucked up during racking.

## Racking and Bentonite Fining

After settling overnight, or even for a day or two, the juice is racked off of its lees into the fermenter, which for home wine-makers is typically a carboy. The juice will foam once fermentation begins, so be sure not to fill the carboy completely. In most cases, you should fill a fermenter less than 90 percent full to leave room for expansion and foam during the peak of fermentation. If logistics dictate that your carboy is only partially full, this is OK, because during the fermentation stage, $CO_2$ will fill the headspace. After fermentation is finished, however, head-space can contain oxygen, which can begin to oxidize the wine.

### Gewürztraminer

Noted for their floral fragrance and spicy flavors, Gewürztraminer grapes are grown in France, Germany, New Zealand, and the United States and prefer cool climates. The wine can be made in styles that range from completely dry to semidry, as well as dessert style.

**Taste characteristics:** distinct spicy, lychee-nut aromas, full-bodied, oily, low-acidity, some bitterness

**Serve:** at 45°F (7°C).

**Pair with:** spicy Asian foods and classic Alsatian and German meat plates.

You can let some air get into the juice during this racking, because the yeast will benefit from the available oxygen. Now is also when we may want to add another fining agent called bentonite. Bentonite is a fine clay that binds with proteins in juice or wine and, like gelatin, eventually drops them to the bottom of the carboy. These proteins can cause haze problems in bottled white wine (it is rarely a problem in reds because the tannins in reds naturally serve the same purpose as bentonite, binding with the wine's proteins). Protein hazing does not affect taste, but it can be unattractive in your glass.

Bentonite is added after settling, because if it is added to cloudy juice, it will bind with the suspended grape solids rather than with the proteins.

**tip**

Young vines ripen their grapes much faster than old vines. The difference can be as much as ten days. Soil differences can also affect ripening times significantly. Thin, well-drained soils ripen grapes faster than heavy, deep soils, even in the smallest parcels.

This protein instability problem is also called heat instability, because it often appears if the wine is warmed (at room temperature, for example).

Just as with gelatin fining, you want to add bentonite to the juice rather than to the wine, because it has the potential to strip wine. Recommended amounts to use are approximately 0.5 to 1 gram per gallon (0.1 to 0.25 grams per liter). You'll need to prepare the bentonite the day before so it has a chance to fully rehydrate and expand. Mix it with hot water at a rate of about 1 gram of bentonite to 1/2 to 1 ounce of water (1 gram to 20 to 30 ml water). Add it to the juice when you rack the clear juice off of its lees into the clean carboy that will become your fermenter. The wine will then ferment in contact with bentonite.

## Fermentation

In most cases, white wines should ferment slowly to retain fruity aromas and freshness on the palate. The rate of fermentation is determined by temperature and the type of yeast strain you use. As a rule of thumb, slow fermentations last about thirty days, moderate about two weeks, and fast fermentations about a week. Slow fermentations preserve more fruitiness

# A Sampling of Yeast Types

## LALVIN WINE YEASTS

| Strain | Whites | Roses | Reds | Ferm Speed | Alcohol Tolerance | Temp Range |
|---|---|---|---|---|---|---|
| BM45 | 2* | 1 | 4 | moderate | 16% | 18–28° C |
| CY3079 | 4 | 2 | 1 | moderate | 15% | 15–25° C |
| EC1118 | 4 | 2 | 2 | fast | 18% | 10–30° C |
| ICV-D21 | 3 | 1 | 4 | moderate | 16% | 15–28° C |
| ICV-D254 | 4 | 1 | 4 | moderate | 16% | 12–28° C |
| R2 | 4 | 3 | 1 | moderate | 16% | 10–30° C |
| T73 | 1 | 1 | 4 | moderate | 16% | 18–35° C |

*Numbers indicate rating: 4 is highest rating, 1 is lowest
(Continued on following page.)

# A Sampling of Yeast Types (Continued from previous page)

## RED STAR YEASTS

### SENSORY EFFECT

| Wine Types | Côte des Blancs | Flor Sherry | Montrachet | Pasteur Champagne | Pasteur Red | Premier Cuvée |
|---|---|---|---|---|---|---|
| Red | ● | | ● | ● | ● | ● |
| Blush | ● | | | | | |
| White | ● | | ● | ● | | ● |
| Sparkling | ● | | | | | ● |

### SENSORY EFFECT

| | Côte des Blancs | Flor Sherry | Montrachet | Pasteur Champagne | Pasteur Red | Premier Cuvée |
|---|---|---|---|---|---|---|
| Fruity Esters | ● | | | | | |
| Aldehydes | | ● | | | | |
| Full-Bodied | | | ● | | ● | |
| Neutral | | | | ● | | ● |

### OTHER CHARACTERISTICS

| | Côte des Blancs | Flor Sherry | Montrachet | Pasteur Champagne | Pasteur Red | Premier Cuvée |
|---|---|---|---|---|---|---|
| Vigorous Fermenter | | | ● | ● | ● | ● |
| Ferment to Dryness | | | ● | ● | ● | ● |
| Restart Stuck | | | | ● | | ● |
| Ethanol Tolerant | | ● | | ● | | ● |
| SO$_2$ Tolerant | ● | ● | ● | ● | ● | ● |
| Low Foaming | ● | | | | | ● |

NOTE: Not all varieties of Red Star and Lalvin yeasts are represented in these charts, nor are all yeast brands represented.

in the wine. Faster fermentations give the wine more richness and a yeasty character.

I recommend using a slow-fermenting yeast strain, because more often than not, the home winemaker does not have the luxury of precise temperature control during fermentation. Examples of commercially available slow-fermenting yeasts are Epernay 2 and Lalvin CY3079. Add these yeasts after rehydrating them in warm water for twenty minutes. Simply pour them on the surface of the juice. Fermentation should start within a day or two. During white wine fermentation, the only time-consuming job you will have is checking and maintaining temperatures of the fermenting juice.

Temperature has a strong influence on the rate of fermentation and, in turn, the style of the resulting wine. Try to keep the temperature of the fermenting wine below 55°F (13°C) for fruity-style wines and between 55°F and 70°F (13°C and 21°C) for a richer style. An old refrigerator or cool nighttime temperatures are the most convenient ways of keeping your carboy cool. Another method is to place the carboy in a tub of ice water and keep adding ice. (Years ago, I found that plastic jugs or bottles filled with water and then frozen worked well.) Remember that fermentation produces heat, so, even though you may be fermenting in a cool cellar, the temperature of the wine may be much warmer than the ambient temperature. Don't assume that the temperature of the room is the same as the temperature of the fermenting wine.

Add yeast nutrients (see chapter nine) as soon as fermentation begins. Nutrients can help prevent problems with stuck fermentations and $H_2S$ problems. They can, however, increase the rate of fermentation, which is why cooler temperatures can be helpful in preventing an excessively rapid fermentation from volatizing all the wonderful fruit aromas from your white wine.

## ●● Barrel Fermenting

Some wines are oak-barrel fermented. Barrel fermentation can give wines a creamy texture and a sweet, vanilla taste. The flavor and taste of a white wine fermented in oak is much more integrated and harmonious than a wine that is aged only in oak. If you desire some oak influence in your white

---

"*The* point at which the grapes are ripe and must, therefore, be picked is less scientifically quantifiable. This crucial decision is often taken in the light of very detailed measurements of levels of fructose, sucrose, malic acid, tartaric acid, and/or pH, but it is ultimately subjective. Ripeness is more in the mind of the grower rather than at a measurable point on a refractometer."

—Jancis Robinson

*Vines, Grapes and Wines*

wines and are unable to ferment in oak barrels because of volume or cost constraints, an option may be to add oak chips. Be cautious, though: Oak flavors can dominate all other flavors, and I have tasted too many wines ruined by the overuse of oak chips. Overoaked wines are what winemakers refer to as "oak juice." Leave the chips in the fermenting wine for only a few days, until you have more experience in tasting fermenting wine and discerning the level of oak flavors extracted from the chips. Oak flavors can be relatively subtle during fermentation and then come out much more strongly several months later as the wine ages.

## Postfermentation

To determine when alcoholic fermentation is finished, taste the wine for any traces of sweetness, and check the fermentation lock to see if the carbon dioxide produced by active yeast is still bubbling through it. If you see little or no bubbling but still taste sweetness in the wine, you could run the risk of having a stuck fermentation. Try stirring and warming the wine to room temperature, to encourage the yeast to finish its job. If all else fails, try some special strains of yeast on the market that are made to help restart a stuck fermentation.

If you want the wine to undergo malolactic fermentation (see chapter nine), inoculate it with ML bacteria as soon as alcoholic fermentation is finished. Keep the wine at room temperature to encourage the bacteria. Do not rack the wine unless it develops $H_2S$ aromas, and avoid adding $SO_2$ at this time, because ML bacteria are very sensitive to sulfur additions. Because MLF also produces small amounts of $CO_2$, you should see some occasional bubbling in the fermentation lock. If after a few weeks the bubbling stops, you can assume that MLF is finished.

Once the alcoholic and (if desired) malolactic fermentations are complete, rack the wine off its gross lees and add $SO_2$. Racking should take place carefully, unless you detect some off aroma ($H_2S$), in which case, you should allow the wine to pick up some air by letting it splash a bit when it fills the new container. With this one exception, anything done to the wine from now on should be done as anaerobically as possible, meaning that you should avoid having air come in contact with the wine.

Icewine, developed in Germany, is becoming popular in Canada and parts of the northern United States. Waiting for grapes to freeze on the vines is only for winemakers with patience and the willingness to gamble.

Just after fermentation, the wine is saturated with $CO_2$, giving it some buffer against $O_2$ pickup, but over time, it dissipates and leaves the wine even more susceptible to oxygen. At all costs, avoid having a headspace (ullage) of more than 1" (2.5 cm) in any container. This is why you will need many different sized carboys or bottles to accommodate varying volumes of wine.

## ●● $SO_2$ Additions

Once the fermentations have finished, you'll want to make your first $SO_2$ addition to the wine. If you are not 100 percent sure that the wine has completely finished fermenting, wait a week or so before adding sulfur. Never add sulfur to an actively fermenting wine—the $SO_2$ will interfere with both alcoholic and malolactic fermentations. If you are going for a fresh, fruity-style wine, $SO_2$ additions will be on the high side (60 to 80 ppm, or 60 to 80 mg/L). For a richer style of wine, especially those aged on their fine lees (see chapter twelve), a lower addition of 40 to 60 ppm is better.

# Lees

When you rack white wine off of its gross lees, you may want to include a bit of the lees for added flavor and texture. By the end of fermentation, most of the solids have fallen out, leaving the desirable spent yeast cells to settle out last. The top layer of the gross lees contains mostly yeast cells (fine lees) and the bottom mostly grape solids (gross lees). Because it is the yeast cells that are desirable, if you decide to age *sur lie* (on the lees), you may want to take up some of the superficial lees when siphoning.

You now have white wine, but it is still pretty rough and cloudy. We will discuss what happens next in Chapter Twelve, *Élevage*.

*tip*

As a rule of thumb, try to minimize racking white wines and maximize racking young red wines. This is because white wines lose their freshness quickly when exposed to the air during racking. Young red wines, on the other hand, will often become more supple and refined when small amounts of air are introduced during the early aging process.

## Sweet Wines

Any wines with sweetness are risky to make. More precisely, they are risky to bottle. This is because residual sugar in the wine is susceptible to fermentation by any remaining yeast after the wine is bottled. Commercial wineries get around this problem by filtering out the yeast at bottling. Although it is possible for home winemakers to use similar filtration methods, the necessary equipment is rather expensive. An alternative is to use a preservative called potassium sorbate, which can prevent yeast from refermenting sugar. Sorbates are not 100 percent effective and can influence the flavor of wine by giving it a bubblegum aroma. Another alternative is to keep the bottled wine refrigerated and drink it quickly.

Two basic techniques are used for making sweet wines. The first is to stop the fermentation before the yeast consumes all the sugar in the juice. The second is to add back sweetness in the form of juice or cane sugar.

To stop fermentation, chill the fermenting wine. As fermentation progresses and the wine loses sweetness, taste the wine daily. Once you feel that the sweetness level is where you want it, put the carboy in a refrigerator, or, if it is cold enough, outside at night. Temperatures below 40°F (4°C) are usually cold enough to stop fermentation, but don't go too cold, because wine will eventually freeze at about 25°F (–4°C).

After a week of chilling, fermentation will have stopped. Be careful to keep the wine cool, because fermentation can start up again if the wine warms. Racking and adding 100 to 120 ppm $SO_2$ will help keep the yeast at bay. Sweet wines require large amounts of $SO_2$ to keep them from refermenting. The sugar also tends to bind up $SO_2$ quickly, making subsequent additions necessary. Wines made this way tend to remain cloudy and require fairly aggressive fining for clarification (see chapter twelve).

Adding back sweetness in the form of juice, a process invented by the Germans, is known as *sus reserve*. If you would like to make a sweet wine, I recommend freezing a portion of the juice after settling but before fermentation. For an "off dry" wine (1 to 2 percent residual sugar), freeze about 5 to 10 percent of the total juice. For a semisweet wine (2 to 4 percent residual sugar), freeze about 10 to 20 percent. Add this thawed juice back to the wine just before bottling.

It is also possible to add cane sugar to wine at bottling (be careful, because this can also cause the yeast to referment). However, cane sugar does not integrate well with the rest of the wine, which is why most premium wine producers avoid it.

*Oak flavors can be relatively subtle during fermentation and then come out much more strongly several months later as the wine ages.*

*tip*

The best and fastest way to chill a bottle of wine is to place it in an ice bucket filled with two-thirds full of ice and water. Leave it for twenty to thirty minutes.

# *homework*

## The Great "Stickies" of the World

*TO LEARN MORE:* Some of the greatest, most expensive wines produced are very sweet dessert wines, affectionately known as "stickies." With these wines, the winegrowers have taken a great risk to harvest grapes with concentrated, exotic flavors. This concentration is achieved in three ways.

**Botrytis (noble) rot**  Grapes are grown in regions in which botrytis rot is conducive to infecting the grapes late in their ripening cycle. This "noble" rot, as French winegrowers call it, concentrates flavors by dehydrating the berries. Only affected grapes are selectively harvested, berry by berry. As you can imagine, very little juice can be squeezed out of these shriveled grapes. The resulting wines are concentrated, with spicy, honeyed flavors. Like all great dessert wines they require many years of aging. Examples include Tokaji, German Trockenbeer-enauslese, Sauternes, and Coteaux du Layon (Loire).

**Frozen grapes (icewine)**  This technique was discovered in Germany, where it is called Eiswein. Grapes are left on the vine until they freeze (temperatures need to be below 18°F [−8°C]), which typically happens late at night. The frozen grapes need to be picked during the night and transported before they thaw, which they begin to do during pressing. The sweetest, most concentrated juice thaws first, whereas the water in the grapes stays frozen longer. Only the first thawed, concentrated juice is retained to make icewine. The remaining juice makes an easy, pleasant dry or semisweet wine.

Icewines typically are piercingly acidic, with pure, fresh, extracted fruit flavors. Examples include icewines from Germany, Austria, and Canada (Ontario and British Columbia).

**Drying grapes**  Grapes are allowed to partially dry, either on the vine or on mats after picking. This dehydration concentrates sugars and flavors and can also contribute a nutty, caramelized flavor to the wine. The grapes are pressed in late fall, after a month or two of drying. Examples include Jurançon (southwest France), Vin Santo (Italy), and vin de paille (France).

To understand different sweet winemaking styles, taste a wine from each of the above categories. (Because of the cost involved with most of these wines, this will be an optional extra credit homework assignment.)

# Making Red Wines

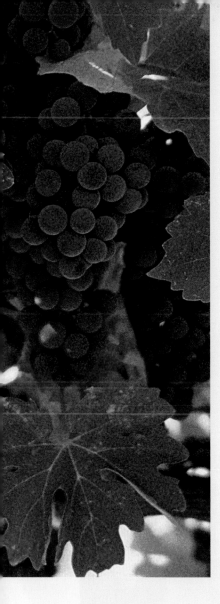

## CHAPTER ELEVEN

*An aged red wine evokes memories, its aromas and flavors eliciting descriptions beyond fruits, flowers, and oak, to remind us of fragrances and experiences of years past.*

*W*hereas white wines are made to be perky and refreshing, red wines should be sensual, on both tactile and emotional levels. "Tactile" refers to mouthfeel—the wine's structure, viscosity, and finish. "Emotional" refers to both the making and enjoying of red wine—intuition, experience, and tradition drive red winemaking more than technology does. An aged red wine evokes memories, its aromas and flavors eliciting descriptions beyond fruits, flowers, and oak, to remind us of fragrances and experiences of years past.

On the surface, it seems easier to make red wine than white wine. The equipment, mechanics, and procedures for making red wine are simple compared to those for white winemaking. Temperatures of grapes, must, and fermentation do not need to be as precise. Pressing is easier and more efficient. And, unlike white wines, red wines naturally clarify and stabilize without the winemaker's intervention. After a year of aging, especially in contact with oak, they become bright and clear, settling out any cloudiness.

It is, however, more difficult to make a great red wine than a great white wine. Despite the easier processes and logistics, picking and fermentation decisions when making red wine are based more on taste and observation than numbers. The biggest difference between red and white winemaking is that when making white wine, you ferment only the juice. To make red wine, you ferment the entire grape. The impact of the skins, seeds, and stems on the resulting wine is enormous—and not measurable by the small-scale winemaker in a lab. It's assessed by taste. Much of the information in this chapter is designed to train your ability to evaluate flavor and mouth-feel qualities like tannins and textures, both in grapes and wine.

# Picking the Grapes

I remember a wine commercial that aired on television in the early 1980s. In it, an Italian grandpa slowly moves through his vines, tasting the grapes, while the rest of the family waits in great anticipation for his verdict on whether it is time to begin the harvest. Back then, I ridiculed the advertisement; as a young winemaker, fully schooled in the importance of measuring Brix, pH, and TA to determine when to pick the grapes (in other words, "picking by numbers"). The idea of making harvest decisions based on taste seemed absurd. Fast-forward a few decades, and we find that most progressive winemakers (including me) are now emulating that grandpa.

## ●● When to Pick

Deciding when to pick is more an intuitive and experiential process than an analytical one. To make good wine, red grapes have to be ripe. Ripeness in red grapes is determined by their flavors and the condition of their skins and seeds.

**Flavors** When red grapes are underripe, they can give off vegetal rather than fruit-based flavors. Although taste is subject to personal preference, most wine drinkers prefer fruit aromas and flavors. (See table, Observing Red Grape Maturity, opposite.)

**Skins** When red grapes are ripe, their skins should be fairly fragile, easily pulling from the pulp and stem. They should stain your fingers when you are out sampling in the vineyard. The grapes themselves should look a bit "tired," meaning slightly dehydrated, not plump and swollen like the ones depicted in all those beautiful still life photos. If the grapes look good, they probably aren't ready to pick.

Skins contain most of the tannins (soluble astringents) that define the quality and style of red wine. Try to get experience in tasting, feeling, and evaluating tannins. I like to take the skins of three or four grapes and gently chew them. Once the sugar is digested, the tannins become apparent. Are they bitter and biting (which means the grapes are not yet ripe), or are they velvety and supple (a great sign of ripeness)? These are good indicators of the texture, structure, and finish you would expect to find in the wine.

*tip*

The temperature at which you serve a wine affects its taste. When a red wine is served too warm, it renders the wine out of balance. A white wine served too cold loses the ability to communicate its aroma. To maximize the flavor of a red wine, serve it slightly chilled— at about 55°F to 65°F (12°C to 18°C).

Unripened seeds can give red wines undesirable, bitter, hard tannins. Unripened seeds are green in color. When deciding when to harvest, look for grapes with ripe seeds—those that are dark brown.

# Observing Red Grape Maturity

Underripe characteristics are never desirable in winemaking. Whether grapes are picked ripe or overripe is an individual stylistic decision. This chart can help you identify the characteristics you want in your wine.

| Grape Maturity | Grape Flavors and Aromas | Grape Skin Tannins | Visual Clues | Wine Characteristics |
|---|---|---|---|---|
| *Underripe* | Herbaceous, canned vegetables, acidic, leafy | Bitter, drying, coarse | Firm, pink berries, green to yellow seeds, little or no pigment on fingers | Thin and biting, light color, vegetable aroma and flavors |
| *Ripe* | Fresh berries, violets, and roses | Dusty, mouth-coating, chewy | soft, juicy berries, brown seeds, slight shriveling, pink to red stains on fingers when sampling | Balanced, structured, complex |
| *Overripe* | Jammy, stewed fruit, prunes | Soft, supple, silky | Lots of shriveling, brittle seeds; red, sticky fingers | Alcoholic, port like, monolithic |

**Seeds**   Seeds also give off tannins. When the seeds are a green to yellow color, they are considered unripe and will contribute harsh, bitter flavors and texture to the wine. The darker their color the better. When deciding if it is time to harvest, you may want to crunch down on some seeds with your teeth. If they are soft, they are not ripe. If they are hard, crunchy, and crack easily, they (and the grapes) are ripe for picking.

# *homework*

## A Matter of Place

***TO LEARN MORE:*** To understand the impact of terroir on wine style, blind-taste two wines made from similar grapes but from different regions: an inexpensive Californian or Australian Cabernet or Merlot, for example, compared to an inexpensive red Bordeaux (typically a Merlot/Cabernet blend). The New World (Californian and Australian) style tends to emphasize flavors of big fruit and supple tannins and often will have a hint of sweetness (residual sugar). The Old World (European) style should be leaner, with less alcohol, and very dry (no apparent sweetness), with less fruit and more earth notes and astringency in its flavor. Taste them before dinner, and then with dinner, to see how your perceptions toward each wine might change.

*tip*

Texture, or mouthfeel, is the most important aspect of red wine. If the vines have been well managed, the yield is kept to low levels, and you pick when the tannins are ripe, not green or biting, you have the foundation for a great red wine. Flavors, aromas, and personality are then defined by the vineyard site (*terroir*), grape variety, and your winemaking decisions.

Pick grapes in the early morning, when they are cool. If the grapes are warm or hot (above 75°F [23°C]), you could run the risk of quick, uncontrolled fermentations. Although it is acceptable to work with warm red grapes, you should be aware that once they are crushed, fermentation will begin quickly, often less than twenty-four hours from crushing.

# Texture Wheel

Terminology for Communicating the Mouthfeel of Red Wine

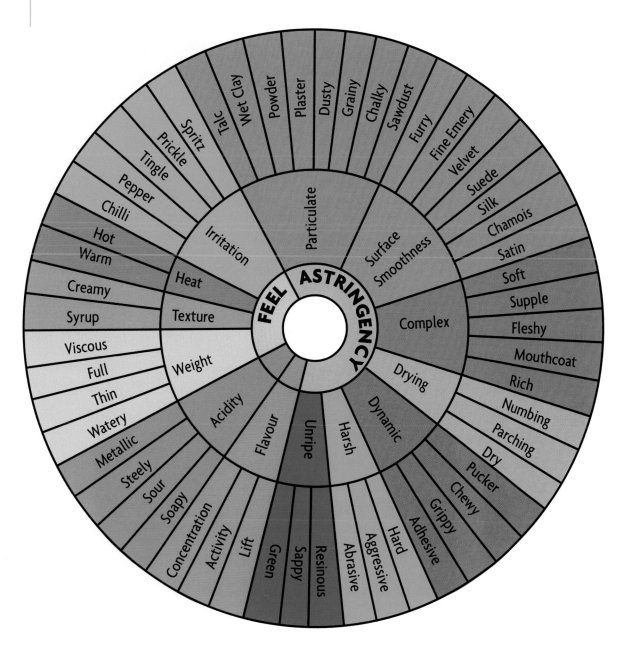

Use this **texture wheel**, reproduced from Richard Gawel et al., © 2000, *Australian Journal of Grape and Wine Research*, to help train your palate to detect the differences in mouth-feel and the qualities of both grapes and wines. The goal is to harvest grapes at the appropriate ripeness to make wines that are supple, velvety, and rich, rather than parching, hard, or green.

## ●● Picking by Numbers

Most experienced winemakers have learned that "picking by numbers" can be detrimental to making high-quality red wines. Tannin and flavor maturity rarely correlate to perfect sugar or acid levels in red-wine grapes. Having said this, it is important to know the Brix and TA levels of the grapes and wine. It is common practice in the winery to adjust these levels, if necessary. Flavors, aromas, and supple tannins, however, cannot be so easily adjusted.

## ●● Brix

Sugar levels of red grapes are usually higher than those of white grapes, primarily because red grapes are picked at later stages of maturity. By the time the flavors and tannins are ripe, the Brix levels can be quite high, in excess of 24°. This high level often works out well, because with more sugar comes more alcohol, and red wines generally carry higher alcohol content better than whites.

The sugar-to-alcohol conversion rate in red wines is generally lower than with white wines. (Because reds ferment at warmer temperatures, more alcohol evaporates, leaving less in the wine.) To determine alcohol levels for reds, I use a Brix-to-alcohol conversion rate of around 0.58. That is, for every degree Brix in the juice, we will get 0.58 percent alcohol in the wine. Juice at 22° Brix, for example, ferments to 12.76 percent alcohol (22 X 0.58 = 12.76). (See chapter eight on measuring Brix and TA levels in grapes.)

Most reds are balanced at a level between 12.5 and 13.5 percent alcohol. However, a trend toward even higher alcohol levels has emerged, because viticultural practices and global warming produce grapes of excessively high sugars (25° to 28° Brix), which ferment into wines of 14 percent alcohol or higher.

**TA** Acid levels of red wines are lower than for white wines. Whites need acidity to give them structure, length of finish, and aging potential, whereas in reds this is accomplished by tannins (contributed by skins and stems). Reds with excessive acid levels tend to taste sharp, thin, and bitter. Typical acidity levels for red grapes are in the range five to eight grams per liter.

# *homework*
ASSIGNMENT

## Concentration Counts

**TO LEARN MORE:** To better understand the significance of grape ripening and the concentration of flavors and sugars on wine style, contrast two wines from the same region and grape variety in which the grapes were picked at different levels of ripeness. Purchase a simple, everyday Valpolicella or Bardolino and an Amarone. All three wines are made from the Corvina grape, but those used for the amarone are picked later and then dried on racks to concentrate the flavors and sugars.

## *tip*

Texture, or mouth-feel, is the most important aspect of red wine. If the vines have been well managed, the yield is kept to low levels, and you pick when the tannins are ripe, not green or biting, you have the foundation for a great red wine. Flavors, aromas, and personality are then defined by the vineyard site (*terroir*), grape variety, and your winemaking decisions.

**pH**    I have not discussed grape or wine pH in much detail, partly because I do not believe that its use is absolutely critical to winemaking, but, more important, because most backyard vintners do not own a pH meter (they are expensive). Some commercial winemakers are concerned that wines with a high pH (above 3.8) will have microbial and aging problems. It is true that a wine's inherent low pH (below 3.6) retards the growth of spoilage organisms and, in fact, is a major preserving factor in wine. Red wines, however, have high levels of tannins, which are antioxidants and help preserve the wine. Some of the great Bordeaux wines have quite high pH levels and are recognized for their long lives.

I don't worry about pH in red grapes. If the levels are very low (below pH 3.2), the grapes are probably not ready to pick, because pH can be an indicator of grape maturity. If the levels are high (above 3.8), I look for signs of premature aging (browning). To compensate, I keep wine SO2 levels higher than normal.

# Sorting, Destemming, and Crushing

Sorting, destemming, and crushing are critical steps in determining wine quality and style. Each step involves quite a lot of time and labor to be done well. This is where some extra hands would be especially helpful—perhaps a good time to recruit some volunteers!

## ●● Sorting

As in white winemaking, the process starts with sorting out rotten grapes or bunches. Fortunately, most red grapes are more rot resistant than white grapes. Rain before and during harvest can, however, result in even the toughest-skinned varieties to rot. If you see pink colored bunches or berries, they should also be discarded because this is a sign of poor ripening. A small amount of unripe grapes in a batch can adversely affect the flavor of the wine.

## ●● Destemming

Most, but not all, red winemakers destem their grapes before fermentation. Stems contribute a significant amount of astringent tannins to the fermenting wines. The decision to include stems and to what degree depends on stem ripeness, grape variety, and wine style. Traditionally, regions that grow lower-tannin grapes, such as Burgundy (Pinot Noir) or the Southern Rhône (Grenache), include some stems in the process. In modern winemaking, the trend is now to meticulously sort out even small stem fragments, known as jacks. Many winemakers feel that the stem tannins are not harmonious with their wine's style, contributing a "greenness" to the wine flavor. Although I lightly chew some stems at harvest to get an idea of the grapes' level of ripeness, I am usually less than enamored of stem flavor.

Modern commercial wineries spend an enormous amount of time, labor, and money to sort out stem fragments. The small-scale vintner will rely mostly on labor. Small-scale mechanical destemmers are on the market, but they are relatively expensive and not very gentle. There is no

*THE FIRST STEP IN MAKING RED WINE is to sort the grapes (a), removing leaves and rotten, pink, or shriveled berries. The next step is to crush the grapes, using one of two methods: by using a crusher/destemmer to remove stems and lightly break the grape skins (b); or by using your feet to lightly break the grape skins (c) and then removing some of the stems by hand. The crushed grapes are left to ferment in an open vat (d). During fermentation, the skins rise to the top of the fermenter and need to be reincorporated into the fermenting wine by "punching down" (e), usually twice a day. After fermenting for about ten days, the wine is pressed from the skins (f). Once the solids have settled overnight, the relatively clear wine is racked into a barrel (g) or carboy for malolactic fermentation and aging.*

# Making Red Wine

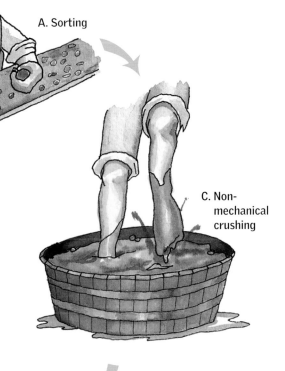

A. Sorting

B. Crushing and destemming

C. Non-mechanical crushing

D. Fermentation

S-bubble-type fermentation lock

E. Punching down

G. Barrel fermenting wine

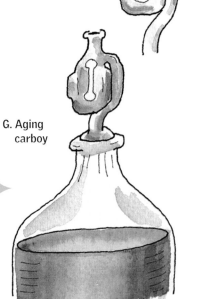

G. Aging carboy

F. Using a basket press to extract wine

substitution for lots of hands plucking berries from the stems. This process can be done before crushing or, on a small scale, just after crushing. You can elect to leave the stems, but be aware that the resulting wine could have a significantly coarse, drying finish (aftertaste).

## ●● Crushing

When crushing, your goal is to lightly and gently break open the skins of the grapes to release the juice and begin the all-important interaction between juice and skins. The amount of crushing you do will have a big impact on the style of the finished wine. If you desire a wine with pretty fruit notes that is soft and appealing for early drinking, you may want to do little crushing. If your grapes have wonderful, ripe tannins that you feel will give power, structure, and longevity to the wine, a more aggressive crushing may be desired. Avoid extreme shredding or pulverizing, because doing so will result in a rapid release of excessively bitter and astringent tannins from both the skins and the seeds. You want only to split open the grapes, not to pulverize them.

Set the crusher over your fermenter (a vat or tub). Remember not to completely fill the fermenter with grapes, because the must's volume will

Using your feet is a very efficient, gentle way of crushing red grapes.

*homework*
ASSIGNMENT

## Beauty Is Skin Deep

**TO LEARN MORE:** To better understand the impact of crushing and skin contact, blind-taste two wines from the same grape and region, but which were made with different levels of skin influence on the fermenting wines. Taste a Nouveau Beaujolais alongside a cru Beaujolais (with a village name such as Morgon or Brouilly). The Nouveau versions are made using a process called carbonic maceration, in which the grapes are not crushed and the wine is bottled only a few months after harvest. Many of the best cru Beaujolais will have more extraction from the skins, which gives the wines more color, structure, and longevity.

expand during fermentation. Leave at least 12" (30.5 cm) of headspace. As a rule of thumb, plan on 8 or 9 lb. of crushed grapes per gallon (1 kg/l) of fermenter space. Lids are not necessary—a simple bed sheet over the top is enough to keep fruit flies out of the fermenting wine.

## ●● Adding SO₂

I recommend adding sulfur dioxide during the crushing operation to temporarily inhibit the activity of spoilage yeast while the desirable yeast begins to multiply. To healthy crushed grapes, add 20 ppm; to crushed grapes with rot, add 50 to 100 ppm. You'll also want to take juice samples at this time, to make sure Brix and TA levels are in an acceptable range. A Brix between 22° to 23° and an acidity of 6 to 7 grams per liter would make most winemakers happy. (See chapter nine for more on adding SO₂.)

# Fermentation

As we learned in chapter nine, to make white wines, we ferment only the juice, leaving the skins, pulp, and seeds out of the process. With red wines, all parts of the grape are included in the fermenter. During fermentation, the skins—and to some degree, the seeds—will greatly influence the color, structure, and flavor of the wine.

Over the past ten years, a trend in red winemaking has been to allow the crushed grapes to soak for several days before fermenting them. This method, called cold soak, was developed in Burgundy as a way of extracting more supple tannins and color stability from the grapes before active fermentation begins. If the temperature of the crushed grapes, or must, is below 55°F (12°C), fermentation should be delayed naturally for two or three days as the crushed grapes slowly warm. Don't let the crushed grapes get too cold for too long (not below 50°F [10°C]), or fermentation will be difficult to get started.

For reds, yeast is added in the same way as for whites: The yeast is rehydrated first, then poured into the must. Red Star Pasteur Red and Lalvin D-254 and EC-1118 are good, all-purpose red wine yeasts.

Add yeast nutrients once fermentation has started, especially if you are not using cultured yeasts. Timing is important. Ideally, add half your

*tip*

The flavor of wine deteriorates when exposed to air, and exposure to heat speeds the deterioration. Recorking opened wine bottles and storing them in the refrigerator can preserve flavor for up to three days. For maximum flavor retention, decant leftover wine into a smaller bottle to reduce its exposure to the air. You can also try filling the bottle with inert gas, available in small canisters from wine shops.

nutrients as soon as you see yeast activity (bubbling or frothing) and the other half one or two days later. By adding nutrients, you might avoid the bane of a stuck fermentation or hydrogen sulfide aromas. Typical rates are around 1 gram per gallon (.25 g/l).

**Adding Oak**   Most red wines benefit from some oak influence during both fermentation and aging. The flavor of oak can add dimension, weight, and structure to red wine. As a purist, I eschew using oak chips or cubes and prefer that the only oak added be in the form of the barrel. Using barrels allows for a slow infusion of oak character and lets small amounts of desirable oxygen enter the wine through the porous wood staves. The small-scale winemaker, however, is at a bit of a disadvantage, because small barrels, unlike the large ones used by wineries, are expensive and, when new, can quickly overwhelm the wine with excessive oak flavors.

Adding a small quantity of oak chips to fermenting red wine is a good way to incorporate subtle, toasty, vanilla flavors. Because the chips are removed during pressing, there is little chance of "overoaking" the wine.

Red wines can integrate oak flavors better than white wines, so if you plan to purchase a small oak barrel, I would recommend using it for red winemaking. Standard-size barrels for commercial winemaking are 59 gallons (225 liters) and require 700 to 800 lb. (300 to 400 kg) of grapes to fill them. Home winemakers can find barrels as small as 5 gallons, but 10- to 30-gallon barrels are more commonly used. If you are making several different lots of red wine, each large enough to fill a barrel, you could rotate each lot every three or four months into and out of one barrel (while the other lots age in glass). This method would be a good way to avoid overoaking one specific lot. (See chapter twelve for more on barrels and barrel aging.)

If using a barrel is impractical, the solution is to use oak chips. However, I recommend using them for fermentation only, not during aging, because there seems to be better integration and a shorter period of exposure to the oak.

## ●● Punching Down

During fermentation, the carbon dioxide produced by the yeast floats the skins to the top of the fermenter, forming what is called the cap. In making red wine, however, you want the skins and the juice to ferment

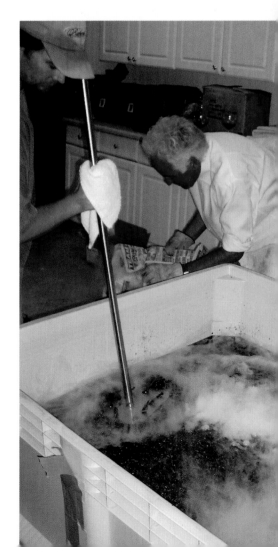

Some winemakers prefer to use their hands when punching down, allowing them to feel temperatures and textures. If you are squeamish about this method, many creative punching-down tools are available. A common tool is a pole with a flat plate attached to it.

As the grape skins float to the top of the fermenter, they should be pushed back, or punched down, into the fermenting wine several times a day.

together, which means that the cap must be pushed down into the fermenting must on a regular basis. This step is known as punching down (*pigeage*). On a commercial scale, punching down is done by hydraulically operated rams; traditionally, it is done by naked men jumping into the vats. This is where the small-scale winemaker has an advantage, because you can simply punch down the cap using your hands. The frequency and degree of punching down will influence the amount of tannins extracted by the fermenting wine. A gentle punchdown, once in the morning and once again in the evening, is typical. After about five to ten days, fermentation will slowly come to an end.

## ●● Must Adjustments

If the vintage is a good one, more often than not you will not have to add anything to your must. However, in all winegrowing regions, at one time or another, winemakers will need to make changes to the sugar or acid levels in their juice or wines. A word of caution: Be very conservative when adding anything to juice or wine. The most common mistake new winemakers make is to overcorrect a deficit, making the problem even worse. If you are not completely sure of how to correct a problem, do nothing.

**Brix**    If the Brix level of the must is too low, cane sugar can be added (see chapter nine to calculate amounts). Many winemakers prefer to add sugar later in the fermentation process; a late addition can prolong fermentation and tannin extraction. Also, it is easier to dissolve sugar in wine than in juice.

In some cases, mostly in California, the sugar level of the must can be too high, which can produce a wine with either residual sugar (the yeast is unable to convert all of the sugar into alcohol) or an excessively high and unbalanced alcohol level (known as a "hot" wine). In these rare cases, the must can be diluted with water to bring down the sugar content. Of course, this water also dilutes all other aspects of the juice and resulting wine.

**Acidity**    Be careful when raising or lowering acid levels in must or wine. I have found this to be one of the most common mistakes made by both professional and home winemakers. How a young wine carries its TA is usually an unknown. It is surprising how a wine seems to adapt, change, and harmonize over time at almost any TA.

If the acidity of the must is too high (see chapter nine), it can be lowered by adding potassium bicarbonate or other similar products. Again, I would caution against this. These kinds of manipulations strip character and leave the wine with a dry, chalky flavor.

If the acidity is too low, an option is to add tartaric acid. If the addition is small and done early, it can integrate into the wine, but often acid additions give a wine's finish a distinct, hard edge. If you feel it is necessary, make additions in small increments and taste-test frequently.

# Pressing

In red winemaking, pressing is the point at which you separate the wine from the skins and seeds. Try to taste the fermenting wine each time you punch it down. You will notice that the wine becomes more astringent with time. This astringency is caused by the tannins being absorbed from the skins and seeds in the fermenting wine. At a certain point you need to make the call: Enough tannins! Time to press.

### ●● **When to Press**

When to separate the wine from the skins is extremely important, in terms of style, because the skins and seeds contribute structure, mouth-feel, and length of finish. Tannin quality and balance are the keys. If the tannins are not ripe, they will contribute "green," or unripe, bitter flavors that will unfortunately define the wine. In this case, an early pressing (short vatting) is advised. Supple, "sweet" tannins are to be cherished and taken advantage of; in this case, long skin-contact time (extended skin contact, or *cuvaisons*) is encouraged.

- **Short vatting** It is surprising how, after only three or four days, a fermenting wine takes on its color and tannin structure. The term "short vatting" comes from Australia, where commercial wines ferment on their skins only until the Brix is at about 15° (about three or four days after the start of fermentation). At this time, the fermenting must is pressed,

*The most common mistake new winemakers make is to overcorrect a deficit, making the problem even worse. If you are not completely sure of how to correct a problem, do nothing.*

Pressing should be done gently and gradually, increasing the pressure on the skins in small increments. A wooden "basket," or cider press, as shown here, is a popular option for home winemakers.

settled overnight, and then racked into oak barrels to finish fermenting.

- **Pressing at dryness** This pressing technique is the most common. The wine ferments on its skins until all of the sugar has turned to alcohol. There is actually a large window here. Often, if the tannins are becoming a bit assertive, the winemaker will press before the fermentation is finished (when there is still detectable sweetness, maybe a week after the start of fermentation), allowing it to finish in a carboy or barrel. Conversely, the winemaker might decide to give a few extra days to the skins' postfermentation, to get a bit more out of the skins.

- **Extended skin contact** This technique is for wine from ripe grapes in which the tannins are emphasized. After fermentation, the vat is sealed, and the wine, skins, and seeds soak for periods of up to thirty days, with the tannins actually softening as they bind together in the vat.

When you're ready to press, gently "bucket" the fermented grapes and wine into the press. A large quantity of juice will be free-run and will not require any pressure. Have an appropriate-sized bucket at the lip of the press tray to catch the flowing wine. Once you begin to press, it is important to taste, because at some point, you will want to put the press wine into a separate container. It can be bitter and astringent and can have vegetal qualities, depending on the vintage. Do not discard it, however. In the winter, when the wines begin to evolve, do some tasting trials to determine whether you want to blend the press wine with the free-run wine.

## *Making Rosé*

You may have noticed more rosés in the marketplace lately. Long condemned as being a girly drink for sissies, it is now cool again to drink rosé. Enough tourists have experienced the epiphany of being in an outdoor café in the south of France, sipping from a cool glass of refreshing, dry rosé, that this bliss is now being re-created in some of the top restaurants worldwide.

An improvement in red wine production is another reason we are seeing more rosé. More winemakers are using a technique called bleeding (*saignée*) for their reds. As the crushed red grapes fill up the fermenter, anywhere from 5 to 20 percent of the juice is drained (bled) from the skins to increase the ratio of skins to the remaining juice. In the event of a rainy harvest, where the vine roots have taken up too much water and pumped up the grapes, the bleeding technique is used to increase the impact of the skins on the juice that remains.

The removed juice, which is used to make rosé, can have varying amounts of color and tannin, depending on the grape variety, the condition of the grapes, and the amount of time that passed between crushing and bleeding. Rosé is fermented and aged just like a white wine, then bottled and consumed early, while it is fresh.

One word of caution, however: Rosés made by bleeding tend to be low in yeast nutrients. When making rosés, it is important to feed your yeast, or you can run into problems with stuck fermentations or hydrogen sulfide aromas.

Although often the only difference between a rosé and a red wine is the amount of time the juice spends in contact with the skins, the wines can be quite different.

*A*n improvement in red wine production is another reason we are seeing more rosé. More winemakers are using a technique called *saignée*.

## Settling

Pressing stirs up lots of lees and skin fragments, which leave the wine cloudy and full of thick, heavy sediment and particles. This gross lees can quickly give off aromas and flavors to the wine, so let freshly pressed wine settle for a day or two before racking it off of its heavy lees. A little bit of air is usually beneficial for new red wines, so when you rack from carboy to carboy or to barrel at this stage, don't be afraid to let the wine splash around a bit.

## Malolactic Fermentation

In malolactic fermentation, lactic acid bacteria are added to convert the wine's malic acid into lactic acid and $CO_2$ (see chapter nine). Unlike white wines, all red wines undergo malolactic fermentation and benefit tremendously from it. MLF enhances mouthfeel, makes the wine more supple, and reduces the need for filtration.

Many strains of ML bacteria are available. I recommend adding it to the wine just after alcoholic fermentation has finished. The yeast may not compete well against the bacteria for nutrients, resulting in a stuck alcoholic fermentation and a wine with sweetness.

MLF needs warm temperatures (between 60°F and 75°F [18°C and 22°C]). While the wine is going through MLF, some $CO_2$ gas is released. The slow bubbling of the fermentation lock is a good indicator of active MLF. An easy test called paper chromatography can show you if there is any more malic acid present in the wine. If the malic acid has not all been converted by the bacteria, there is a good chance they will finish the job the next summer, when the wine temperatures warm. This is why you should wait to bottle, because it is better to have MLF finish in a carboy or barrel than in a corked wine bottle.

Once ML is complete, most winemakers prefer to add between 20 and 50 ppm of $SO_2$ to maintain a level of about 15 to 25 ppm of free $SO_2$. The next step is *élevage*.

# Élevage

## CHAPTER TWELVE

*Élevage* encompasses all the decisions we make from postfermentation until bottling. Your wine is alive and will evolve, often on its own with little help from you.

*N*ow you now have wine, albeit wine that is cloudy, yeasty smelling, and rather innocuous tasting. That's the way it is supposed to be. In many cases, if you do nothing at all from this point on, your wine will settle clear, evolve, and taste great. In some cases, you may want to intervene with the aging of your wine. This is the basis of *élevage*. Loosely translated from the French, élevage means "raising"—"raising" in the way parents would raise their children. The analogy works well, in that some children are easy and well behaved, needing little discipline or guidance, whereas other children need a heavier hand and seem to always be going through a difficult time. In the winemaking sense, élevage encompasses all the decisions we make from postfermentation until bottling. Just remember that one option is to do nothing!

By now, you should have a carboy or barrel filled to the top with your wine. Both alcoholic and malolactic (if desired) fermentations have finished, and SO2 has been added. The wine is cloudy, but you will notice that, over just a few weeks, it will begin to clarify and more lees will form on the bottom. Fermentation locks should be replaced with solid stoppers (known as bungs).

## Pinot Noir

One of the most difficult grapes to grow, Pinot Noir grapes require very specific growing conditions and are difficult to make into great wine. When the winemaker is successful, however, Pinot Noir can be considered one of the very best wines. Pinot Noir grapes are relatively low in tannins and produce wines with healthy acidities, more than you would expect from a red grape.

**Taste characteristics:** cherry and strawberry aromas and flavors

**Serve:** at 50°F to 60° (10°C to 15°C))

**Pair with:** light-bodied Pinot Noir pairs well with grilled seafood, whereas full-bodied Pinots pair well with red meats, beef burgundy, and coq au vin.

## The Aging Process

Every wine and winemaker is different, so there is no exact time frame for élevage. For me, the winter months are the most exciting, because this is when the wines start to unveil their true characters as the wines clear and the aromas evolve. During this time, you may be stirring the lees a few times a month, topping off barrels, and racking red wines every month or two. In the spring, you may consider bottling some of your fruity white wines, but if you do not have filtration (it's expensive), I recommend waiting to avoid having them referment when the temperature rises. Spring is a good time to check sulfur dioxide levels of aging wines and adding $SO_2$, if needed. The wines become more delicate in the spring as they lose their naturally protective $CO_2$, so try to do as little racking, stirring, and sampling as possible. Late summer is for bottling because you will want to empty your carboys or barrels to make room for the new vintage.

*tip*

Procrastination is a grapegrower's worst enemy and a winemaker's best friend.

*"This wine was bottled in the traditional way and may therefore contain a noble and natural sediment at one point in its evolution. This is a sign that the wine is alive, and to prevent the formation of sediment by filtration or by any other means is to take away its life and character."*

*—from the back label of Domain Leroy, Burgundy, France*

## Temperature

Temperature can have an impact on how the wine develops during the aging process. European winemakers discovered long ago that cellars are good places to age wines; over the centuries, they have learned how to take advantage of the cellar's natural temperature fluctuations. During the winter months, cellar temperatures can fall well below 50°F (10°C). These cooler temperatures aid in clarifying the wine and allow for detartration.

Detartration refers to a natural process in which naturally occurring potassium and tartaric acids in the wine combine to form a crystal called potassium tartrate, more commonly called tartrates. Detartration happens under cold conditions. Many commercial winemakers chill their wines down to about 30°F (–1°C) to encourage detartration to happen in the winery rather than in the bottle, when the wine is chilled in a refrigerator at a restaurant or at home. When it does happen in the bottle, very fine crystals will attach to the cork or float in the wine. Winemakers refer to this as "snowing in the bottle"; German winemakers call them "wine diamonds." Tartrates are not harmful nor do they affect flavor (except to very slightly reduce the wine's acidity). If you have bought enough wines from artisan winemakers, you have probably come in contact with tartrates.

Some producers feel that the very cold temperatures necessary to cold-stabilize their wines can be harmful to the wine, because wines absorb more oxygen when they are cold. Not cold-stabilizing wines is one example of noninterventionist winemaking. The winemaker decides to do nothing, knowing that the consequences could be crystals showing up in the bottled wine. If you are concerned about having tartrates in your bottled wine, chill your wine in carboys down to 28°F to 32°F (–2°C to 0°C) for a few weeks. This should cause most of the tartrates to fall out.

As summer warms the cellar to 60°F (15°C) or more, some wines may "come alive" again and begin to progress with any unfinished alcoholic or malolactic fermentations that have been stimulated by the warmer temperatures. Just let these processes continue to completion. Pressure from refermentation can blow off a solid bung or stopper, so replace it with an air lock. Once finished (no more pressure in the air lock), the wine will again settle clear.

## Lees

Aging wine on its fine lees can give a wine more depth, creamy texture, and complexity. Lees can also act as a buffer to oxidation. Wines aged on their lees typically require less SO2. One winemaking practice is called *batonnage*: stirring the wine to get more lees impact. The thinking here is that if the lees are in suspension, they will have a greater flavor impact than if they are simply sitting on the bottom of the carboy or barrel. In commercial wineries, batonnage is done by opening up the barrel bung and using a device that looks like a golf club to gently whip the bottom of the barrel. Home winemakers have the advantage here, because with smaller containers, you can stir up the lees by shaking or rotating a carboy or barrel. You also avoid subjecting the wine to much air by not having to open the bung.

As with so many winemaking decisions, there is no formula for the amount of time wine ages on the lees or for stirring regimes. Chardonnay is commonly given the full treatment, aging and stirring through the winter into early spring, whereas more aromatic wines such as Sauvignon Blanc and Riesling tend to receive less lees stirring. Traditionally, red wines were not aged on their lees, but a trend has developed to age reds sur lie with frequent batonnage, reflecting a desire by some winemakers to make wines that are more full bodied and supple.

## Barrel Aging

Aging in oak barrels is common practice for most commercial wineries. Unfortunately, because of scale (a lack of volume), this can be difficult for the home winemaker. The standard-sized wine barrel holds 225 liter, or fifty nine gallons. During aging, the barrels must be completely full. This is quite a lot of wine, especially of one type, for the home winemaker. Smaller barrels are available and can be used, but, as previously noted, there are certain disadvantages to these.

The first disadvantage is expense. Barrel prices do not decline commensurate with volume. If a 59-gallon (225-liter) French oak barrel costs U.S. $800, a 30-gallon (110-liter) size would cost about U.S. $500, whereas a 5- to 8-gallon (19- to 30-liter) size will cost about $200.

> "*C*oopering a barrel can be done only by hand and is a very labor-intensive task. This is why a small barrel can cost almost as much as a large one."

# *Zinfandel*

Also known as Primativo, Zinfandel is at home in California. Zinfandels range in style from fruity blush wines, to fresh early drinking reds, to almost portlike reds. Zinfandel is a great example of how terroir influences and winemaking techniques can make totally different wines from the same grape variety.

**Taste characteristics:** fruit flavors, with spicy overtones

**Serve:** red Zinfandel should be served at cellar temperature (60°F[15°C]); white Zinfandel should be chilled, at white wine temp

**Pair with:** Red: duck, lamb, chorizo sausage, other spicy, full-flavored meats

**White:** ethnic foods, such as Indian, Asian, Caribbean, and Mexican

The second disadvantage is flavor impact. The smaller the barrel, the greater the surface to volume ratio, resulting in oak flavors that overwhelm the grape flavors. Simply put, it is very easy to overoak wine in small barrels. I've known home winemakers to age in small oak barrels for only a few weeks before removing the wine because of excessive oak flavors.

The third disadvantage is oxygen impact. Aging wine in barrels allows a small amount of oxygen into the wine. For a 59-gallon barrel, the amount of $O_2$ pickup is considered ideal for aging reds and some whites. But because of the surface-to-volume ratio of small barrels, the wine can pick up too much $O_2$.

The fourth concern is with maintaining empty barrels. Glass, stainless-steel, and plastic containers need only a good cleaning before storing them indefinitely without worry. Oak barrels are a different story. Their porosity and rough surface makes them virtually impossible to adequately clean. Wine will remain hidden in the wood of oak barrels even when they are "empty," allowing spoilage organisms to grow and spoil the barrel. For this reason, barrels need to be either stored full of water with a potassium metabisulfite–and–citric acid solution to prevent microbial growth or to be treated regularly with the burning of sulfur sticks.

Storing barrels with water alone results in "funky" microbial growth in the water and, therefore, the barrel. You will need to add SO need to the water, at the rate of at least 200 ppm, along with citric acid (1 tablespoon per gallon [2 to 4 grams per liter]). This solution should be changed every few months. Be aware that the solution will leach out some of the oak flavor components of the barrel, which may or may not be a concern, depending on how much oak flavor you would like to impart on the wine you will subsequently be aging in the barrel.

The other method of storing empty barrels is to burn a sulfur stick in them. This method is centuries old. Available at winemaker supply shops, sulfur sticks are somewhat like very large, slow-burning matches. A stick is lit and then inserted in the barrel, burning the inside the barrel for ten or fifteen minutes. The sulfur gas produced by the burning prevents microbial growth from forming on the interior staves. This process should be repeated on a monthly basis.

When storing empty oak barrels over long periods (several months or more), they can dry out and lose their ability to hold wine. This is especially true in dry climates. Before putting wine in a barrel that has been empty for more than a few weeks, it is a good idea to fill it first with water. If there are leaks, the water will swell the wood, and usually within a day or two, the leaks will stop. Better to have water leaking on the floor than wine!

## Topping Off

Topping off is necessary for wine in any container, but it is done primarily to wines aging in oak barrels. Barrels lose wine to evaporation through the wood staves, especially in low humidity. This loss is referred to as the "angel's share." It can amount to four to eight percent of the wine's volume per year. If the barrel bung is removed for sampling, oxygen

*tip*

Mood and environment can influence your impression and evaluation of wine. When making important blending or fining decisions, I like to taste the wines on several occasions, with different people and in different places.

*homework*
ASSIGNMENT

## To Blend or Not to Blend

**TO LEARN MORE:** Many new-world wineries make a blend of Bordeaux grape varieties often called a Meritage. Try to purchase a winery's Meritage along with their Merlot, Cabernet Sauvignon, and/or Cabernet Franc. Try to get all the wines from the same winery and the same vintage, to make fair comparisons. This way you can taste blended and nonblended wines that should demonstrate the balance and complexity of blending versus the varietal character of single-grape wines.

# Common Fining Agents

| Agent | Description | Use | Rate | Comments |
|---|---|---|---|---|
| *Bentonite* | Fine, colloidal clay powder | clarification & protein stabilization | 1–2 g/gallon (0.25–0.5 g/l) | mix in hot water 1 day before using |
| *Gelatin* | powder or liquid from skin & bones of cattle | white juice and young white wines to remove bitterness | 0.06–0.5 ml/gal (0.015–.125 ml/l) or 0.5–1.0 g/gal (0.125–0.25 g/l) | can strip wines; often counter-fined with Bentonite |
| *Egg Whites* | fresh, mixed with a pinch of salt | red wines only; gives supple finesse to finish | 2–8 egg whites per 60-gal (225-l) barrel; 1/2 egg white per 5-gal (19-l) carboy | mix gently, do not whip eggs |
| *Isinglass* | powdered swim bladder of sturgeon fish | delicate white wines; removes bitterness; gentle to wine | 0.01–0.1 g/gal (0.0025–0.025 g/l) | mix with cold water; does not settle well |
| *Casein* | powdered skim milk: potassium caseinate | clarifies white wines and reduces oxidized flavors & aromas | 1–2 g/gal (0.25–0.5 g/l) | can substitute store-bought, powdered milk |
| *Sparkolloid* | proprietary, alginate based | clarifies white wines, neutral flavor | 0.5–1.5 g/gal (0.125–0.4 g/l) | hot mix and cold mix formulations available |

## *Blending in Bordeaux*

The red wines of Bordeaux are blends of two or more grapes. Even more specifically, wines from the Medoc region, producer of most of the classified growths in Bordeaux, are usually blends of three or four grapes. Over the centuries, Bordelais winemakers have learned that different grape varieties have specific soil and climate preferences, that each grape variety can contribute different flavor and structure profiles, and that the weather in each growing season can be variable, affecting the quality and taste of each grape variety in a different way.

The wines of the Medoc are blends that almost always include Cabernet Sauvignon and Merlot, and usually contain some Cabernet Franc and occasionally a bit of Petit Verdot. The reason for this diversity is that each wine made from these grapes contributes different strengths and weaknesses. Blending them creates a more complete wine.

Examples of each grape's character follow:

**Cabernet Sauvignon**  Provides the foundation of the blend with fine, long-lasting tannins. It can have slightly herbaceous flavors, and it sometimes lacks body and flesh (mid-palate weight).

**Merlot**  Makes a very soft, round wine with ripe fruit aromas. It nicely fills the "holes" of the Cabernet Sauvignon.

**Cabernet Franc**  Makes a very aromatic wine. It gives perfume to a blend, but, like Cabernet Sauvignon, it can be fairly herbaceous.

**Petit Verdot**  Makes a rustic, dense, darkly colored wine that can be too assertive on its own but in very small amounts, can give a blend color and body.

Many other winegrowing regions, from Italy and Australia to California, are emulating the Bordelais blending concept. In the United States, winemakers have given the Bordeaux-style blend the name "Meritage."

will fill the headspace, making it necessary to refill the barrel to the top with wine. Remember that in all cases, wine containers have to be filled. If you are aging wine in oak barrels, it is a good idea to keep several small bottles of your wine in the cellar to use as topping wine when needed.

## Sulfur Dioxide

$SO_2$ levels need to be monitored and maintained during aging, and for this I highly recommend purchasing Chemetrics' $SO_2$ kit to measure the levels of $SO_2$ in your wine. See the chart in chapter nine) for the recommended $SO_2$ levels during aging for various wine styles.

## Fining

Briefly discussed in chapter ten, fining is the temporary addition of a material to wine (or juice) to clarify, stabilize, or modify the taste or aroma of the wine. Once this material falls to the bottom of the container, the clear wine is racked off of the fining lees. It is not necessary to fine wine, but understanding how fining agents work can help you solve problems such as a wine that will not clarify naturally or a wine that remains bitter in the finish. All of the fining agents listed in the chart on page 151 can help clarify a cloudy wine. However, each fining agent has characteristics that may be more appropriate in certain situations. For example, egg whites are commonly used in red wines, because they help stabilize color and soften tannins. These attributes are not needed with white wines.

## Blending

As your wines age, you should taste and become familiar with them. If you have different batches or lots, it is a good idea to taste them blind (tasting without knowing which wine you are tasting). Make notes as you taste. You may find that certain lots are not as harmonious as you might like. If bitter, they might be good candidates for fining. If the acidity or tannins are out of balance, blending can be a good way to make two disjointed wines into a wine that is more harmonious. This is what we call 1 + 1 = 3. A synergy takes place that can be measured only by your palate. This is one of the arts of winemaking. This is also why making wines is very individualistic. Everyone's palate preferences are different.

If you plan to try blending wines, first perform some trials. In the winter, once the wines have settled, take small samples (3 or 4 ounces [100 ml]) of each wine you are considering, blend them, and taste the results.

# Bottling

## CHAPTER THIRTEEN

*B*ottling wine is a simple and satisfying task. Once done, you feel a great sense of wealth and pleasure at seeing all those bottles. But before we get to the details of bottling, two principal concerns need to be addressed: ensuring that the wine does not referment in the bottle, and that only a small amount of oxygen is picked up by the wine during bottling.

If wine referments in the bottle, it becomes fizzy ($CO_2$ is produced) and cloudy. Flavor and aroma profiles change, and the corks could push out because of the $CO_2$ pressure. In a worst-case scenario, you could have wine leaking all over the floor. Wine can referment in the bottle if it is sweet (remaining yeast ferments the residual sugar) or if it has malic acid (it begins malolactic fermentation). Even if the wine is perfectly clear, it will contain yeast and bacteria.

*T*aste your newly bottled wine every few weeks to evaluate how it is progressing. You'll be surprised at its evolution.

# SO₂ Levels at Bottling

Knowing your wine's SO₂ levels is most critical at bottling. If a given wine's SO₂ level is too low, the wine can quickly oxidize and be more susceptible to refermentation if traces of malic acid or fermentable sugars remain. If levels are too high, the wine can take on a burnt-match aroma and not develop in the bottle. A guide to recommended free SO₂ levels in different wine styles follows. These levels should be present in your wine just before bottling. If you need to add potassium metabisulfite to the wine to achieve these levels, refer to the calculations in chapter nine.

Reds, 15 to 25 ppm

Dry whites, 25 to 35 ppm

Sweet winesor whites with malic acid, 40 to 60ppm

## ●● Wines with Residual Sugar

No completely accurate method of testing for fermentable sugar is available to the home winemaker. Your best options are to depend on your own palate or use a simple test such as Clinitest, which tests blood-sugar levels in diabetics, available from most winemaking suppliers. These tests typically use color-change indicators as a measurement. You will need to match different shades and tones of colors to determine the sugar level in your wine. Obviously this process is rather subjective. If your wine does have residual sugar, I recommend waiting until after the first summer to bottle it.

If you do bottle wines with sweetness, I recommend storing the wine under cool conditions (below 50°F [10°C]) to avoid stimulating the yeast. Potassium sorbate, a preservative available from most winemaking supply shops, can help prevent the refermentation of sugar. It is not 100 percent effective, however, and can impart a bubblegum flavor to the wine.

## ●● Wines with Malic Acid

A fairly simple and inexpensive test called paper chromatography can test for the presence of malic acid in wine, available from most winemaking suppliers. If your wine does contain malic acid, it will be susceptible to MLF in the bottle. High SO₂ levels at bottling and

Most home winemakers start with a simple siphon tube for bottling, but it is possible to purchase some fairly sophisticated small filtration/bottling units.

# Bottling

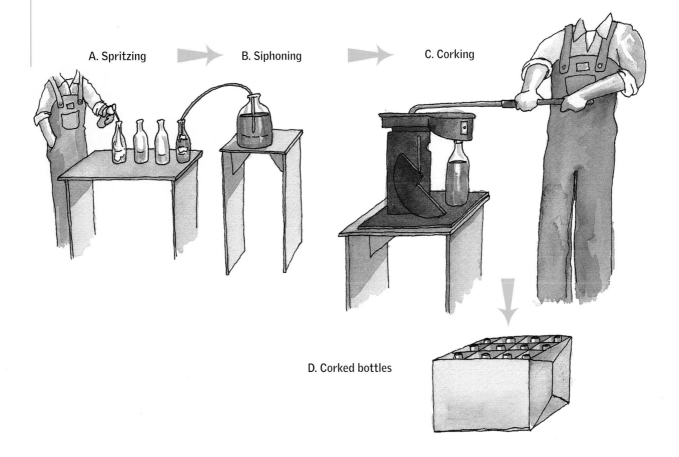

A. Spritzing → B. Siphoning → C. Corking

D. Corked bottles

*Bottling can be fun if you have lots of help! Using an assembly-line method helps to move each stage of the process along quickly and efficiently.*

*Start with clean, dry bottles (use a bottle stand for this). Spritz each bottle with an inert gas, such as $CO_2$, $N_2$, or a blend—canisters of these gases are available at wine shops (a). To fill the bottles, place one end of a small-diameter siphoning tube in the carboy and, once you have the wine flowing, the other end into the bottle (b). Be sure to position the tube all the way to the bottom of the bottle, to prevent splashing. Once each bottle is filled, cork it (c), using new corks to ensure a good seal. Corking can require some stamina, especially if you have a lot of bottles. If you choose, you can then place decorative capsules and labels on the bottles. Place the bottles upright in their cases for a few weeks, to allow the pressure from corking to dissipate (d). Then turn the bottles upside down—the wine keeps the cork from drying out.*

# A Word about Bottles

Wine bottles come in a variety of shapes and colors, and while, as a backyard vintner, you may not be concerned with the type of bottle in which you place your wine, certain bottle shapes are traditionally used for specific types of wine. Bottle shape and color is a kind of shorthand that wineries use to communicate wine type to their consumers.

Bottles also come in varying sizes. The standard wine bottle is 750 ml, but half-bottles (375 ml) are also available, as are 187-ml bottles. Larger sizes, ranging from 1.5 liters to as much as 15 liters, can also be purchased. These can be quite expensive, may require special corkers, and are not for everyday use.

## Bordeaux Bottle

The Bordeaux bottle has high shoulders and is used primarily for wines made from the region of Bordeaux or from grapes that originated in Bordeaux. White wines are usually bottled in clear bottles; green bottles are used for red wines.

## Burgundy Bottle

The Burgundy bottle is slope-shouldered and is most often used for Chardonnay and Pinot Noir wines, from the Burgundy region of France. It is also used for many wines from the Loire Valley. High-quality Burgundy bottles are a dead-leaf green color.

## Hock Bottle

Most commonly used for German wines, the Hock bottle is slim with long, sloping shoulders and is green (for Mosel wines) or brown (for Rhine wines). It is also used in Alsace. Wineries use the Hock bottle for Riesling, Gewürztraminer, and Muller-Thurgau wines.

cool storage conditions will greatly reduce the chances of this happening.

A sterile filtration of the wine can remove all bacteria and yeast at bottling and greatly reduce the chance of refermentation. Unfortunately, it is impractical on a home scale, because of the high cost of the filters and pumps required.

## The Bottling Process

Oxygen pickup is the primary concern during bottling. Most wines are fairly fragile by bottling time. They have lost their natural $CO_2$ protection and have developed delicate aromas and flavors that are susceptible to fading if they come in contact with too much air. I strongly recommend the use of an inert gas ($CO_2$, nitrogen, or the now widely available "wine preserver" canisters. Use new bottles and thoroughly clean them before use (see illustration, directional). Fill the bottles with gas just before siphoning the wine into the bottle, to reduce $O_2$ pickup. When siphoning, fill the bottles slowly, with minimum flow, and put the end of the siphon hose at the bottom of the bottle to reduce splashing. Leave about 1/2" (1.5 cm) of headspace between the wine and the cork.

### ●● Corking

Several types of corkers are available. I recommend the floor models, which are easy to use. To use one, put the bottle in place, then insert the cork into the corker's jaws. When you pull down the handle, the jaws compress the cork so it fits into the bottle's neck, and the plunger rod forces the compressed cork into the bottle. Always buy new corks; do not try to reuse old ones, because they will have been compressed for too long and will not form a tight seal.

Once the wine is corked, you may want to store the bottles upright for a day or two, because the wine will be under a bit of pressure from the corking. Storing the wine upright allows the pressure to dissipate through the cork. You will then want to store your wine either on its side or upside down, to ensure that the cork stays moist from the wine and does not dry out. (See "Closures" for more on corks and their alternatives.)

## ●● Bottle Aging

Bottling can be a bit rough on wine. Winemakers often speak of "bottle sickness." This is when the wine closes down or goes mute; that is, it loses some of its flavor and aroma. The wine can also become disjointed. It may have tasted balanced and harmonious just before bottling, but just after bottling, all its warts seem to appear. The acids taste hard, and the wine's body seems to have disappeared, making the wine taste thin. Likely causes are all the possible manipulations ($SO_2$ additions, fining, filtering, $O_2$ pickup) done to the wine just prior to bottling. If bottle sickness occurs, your wine will revive with time. Sometimes, wines need a few months to revive, sometimes even longer. Taste your newly bottled wine every few weeks to evaluate how it is progressing. You'll be surprised at its evolution.

The conditions in which you age your wines are very important, especially if you plan on aging them for years, rather than months. The two critical factors are cool temperatures and absence of light. Ideal temperatures are in the range of 50°F to 60°F (10°C to 16°C). Avoid heat (more than 80°F [26°C]), because your wine can quickly "cook." Wine does not like light, especially direct sunlight. If you do not have dark conditions, I recommend aging your wines upside down in closed cardboard case boxes.

Probably one of the biggest unknowns for a new backyard vintner is how your wines will age. There is no way of knowing, except to age them and taste. Don't drink or give away all your wine immediately. Save some bottles, so that you have a library of wines and vintages to evaluate what time does to your wines.

As wine ages in the bottle, it often evolves. It "knits" together, becoming more harmonious and seamless. It gains complexity. New, subtle aromas and flavors slowly appear. When a wine is

A corker is absolutely necessary if you use new corks (highly recommended). To use a corker, insert the cork into the "jaws," place a bottle below it, and pull the lever down. The jaws compress the cork, and a plunger forces the compressed cork into the neck of the bottle. It can take a little practice to ensure that the cork goes straight into the bottle.

When bottling, fill just into the neck of the bottle, so that, once corked, there is no more than 1/2" (1 cm) of space between the wine and the cork.

## *Closures*

Although natural cork is still the overwhelming favorite wine closure for most winemakers, there has been interest in finding alternatives because cork has two problems: it can leak, and it can impart off flavors into the wine.

Leaking is not a huge issue. When it happens, it usually happens within a few days of storing the bottles on their sides or upside down. You might find one bottle out of several hundred that leaks. A "leaker" bottle is a great candidate to sample and share with friends.

Off flavors can also develop over time. When this happens, we refer to the wine as being "corked." A distinct, musty, wet-cardboard aroma is the signature of a corked wine. This is one of the reasons you should always smell a wine before it is served at a restaurant. If the wine has the musty, corked aroma, you have good reason to refuse the bottle and ask for another. The cork industry has been working on this problem, with some success, because we seem to be smelling corked wines less frequently. The industry average for corked wine is roughly two to four percent.

Synthetic corks avoid the corked problem, but there have been significant leakage issues with these, especially if the corker is out of alignment. I would be a bit hesitant in recommending them to home winemakers.

Screw caps are also becoming more common commercially and are perfectly acceptable as a wine closure. The industry is still unsure of how wines will age over the long run using screw caps, but for early-consumption whites, they have proven themselves. If you use screw caps, be prepared for snide comments from your friends when you ceremoniously open a bottle of your pride and joy.

young, it has lots of primary aromas and flavors. ("Primary" refers to the fruitiness derived from the grape.) Winemaking practices such as stirring the lees or adding oak contribute to secondary aromas and flavors that increase in intensity over time. Tertiary aromas and flavors develop only with significant bottle aging, and it often takes years of bottle aging for these compounds to evolve. Mushrooms, tar, Asian spices, leather, and lead pencil are some examples of the earthy and mineral (terroir) aromas that can develop with time.

## Capsules and Labels

You can capsule and label your wine after bottling. Capsules (the caps that are slipped over the bottle tops) are purely decorative and serve no practical purpose. Most commercial wineries use tin spin-on capsules, but the machine to apply them is expensive. I recommend plastic heat-shrink

# *homework*
ASSIGNMENT

## Understanding Wine Aging

*TO LEARN MORE:* Try to put together a vertical tasting of the same wine—that is, a tasting of several different vintages of the exact same wine. I recommend choosing a red wine from Bordeaux, Rhône, Burgundy, Piedmont (Italy), or Tuscany. Try to find a current release (young), a wine that is about five or six years old, and one that is ten years old or older. You may have to do some legwork on this project, because only a few specialty wine shops in metropolitan areas will have anything like this available. The Internet is actually your best bet. (See Resources, page XXX.)

### *tip*

There are no secrets in winemaking, but if there were, top on the list would be understanding and using lees. Healthy lees contribute a texture, richness and complexity that define great wine.

Capsules are purely decorative and come in a variety of colors, to match your bottles or your labels. Heat-shrink capsules are easily applied and need no special equipment.

capsules that are attractive, commonly available, and can be applied without purchasing any equipment. A powerful blow dryer or stove top can work. Computers can make labels easy to design and print, whereas winemaking supply catalogues often provide custom labels at a price that might be discouraging. They also sell the glue to apply labels.

# Conclusion

Don't think that your work is done once you have wine in the bottle. All great winemakers are driven to do better. *"Jamais content"* (never content): this philosophy focuses us to critique our own efforts and to learn and evolve as winegrowers. Be your own best (or worst) critic. Find the flaws in your wines. Taste yours alongside others of similar style. Have others with experienced, subjective palates taste your wine. Enter wine competitions that give you verbal feedback, not just numbers or awards. If you want accolades, have your mother taste your wine.

The premise of this book is to help you develop a critical, experienced palate and then depend on that palate to make decisions. Once wine-makers have lots of their own wine, they can easily fall into the "cellar palate" trap—when a winemaker only drinks his or her own wine. They stop learning and become stale. Keep buying wine. Give yours away to friends and family.

Finally, I've written about balance in reference to wines, but balance can also be applied to ourselves. We need to know when to taste wine and when to enjoy wine. There is a difference. Throughout this book I have only referred to tasting for information. This is what progressive winemakers do, but this is not why wine exists. Wine is for drinking and for enhancing food and conversation. Wine gives us pleasure. It slows us down, and it makes us happy. This is wine's job.

*Salut!*

*B*e your own best (or worst) critic. Find the flaws in your wines. Taste yours alongside others of similar style. The premise of this book is to help you develop a critical, experienced palate and then depend on that palate to make decisions.

# Glossary of Winemaking Terms

**Alcoholic fermentation**—The process by which active yeast changes sugar into alcohol. Many other flavor and texture changes also occur. Referred to as simply fermentation.

**Balance**—In wine, when all the individual components harmonize, so that no one aspect of the wine (that is, acid, alcohol, oak, tannins) overwhelms the others.

**Barrel**—Refers specifically to a wooden (usually oak) barrel. The standard size is 59 gallons (225 liters), but much smaller sizes are available.

**Brix**—(degrees Brix, or °Brix) Percentage of sugar in must, expressed in degrees.

**Cap**—During red-wine fermentation the skins will float to the top of the fermenter, forming a cap. This cap needs to be mixed into the fermenting wine.

**Carboy**—A large glass bottle (usually 3 to 5 gallons [11 to 19 l] in size) that can be used to ferment white wines and to age both reds and whites.

**Crush**—a) The light and gentle breaking of the grape's skin. b) The busy period of time in the fall that includes harvesting, crushing, pressing, and fermenting the grapes.

**Dryness**—The point at which all the fermentable sugar in the must has changed to alcohol and fermentation stops.

*Élevage*—The winemaking period from after fermentation until bottling. There is no exact English translation, but the words raising and upbringing are close. During this stage (also known as aging), the winemaker may choose to intervene or simply let the wine evolve on its own.

**Fermenter**—Container in which juice ferments into wine. White wines generally ferment in glass carboys. Red wines, which ferment in their skins, are usually fermented in open-top, plastic containers, such as large buckets.

**Lees**—The sediment that forms over time as small pieces of yeasts and grape skins settle to the bottom of the carboy or barrel.

**Malolactic fermentation**—The process by which bacteria convert the grape's natural malic acid into lactic acid. This process reduces the wine's acidity and the possibility of it refermenting in the bottle.

**Must**—Grape juice (for white grapes) or crushed grapes, including the skins, juice, and seeds (for red grapes).

**Oxidation**—Browning of juice must or wines from contact with oxygen.

**Pressing**—Separating the juice or wine from the grape skins by pressing down on them. This process is done with a press.

**Punching down**—The process of resubmerging the cap into the fermenting wine.

**Racking**—The process of transferring juice or wine from one container to another. For the small-scale vintner, this is usually done with a siphon tube.

**Stuck fermentation**—When must stops fermenting before all the sugar has been converted to alcohol.

**Style**—A flavor and texture profile in a wine that gives it personality. Examples of styles are: light, crisp, and refreshing; weighty, complex, and mouth-filling; fruity, simple, and pleasant.

**Sulfur**—Also referred to as $SO_2$, or sulfur dioxide. A preservative added to juice and wine to prevent excessive browning (oxidation) and to slow down the development of undesirable micro-organisms.

**Tannins**—Naturally occurring compounds found in grapes that contribute astringent and/or bitter tastes to wine.

**Vintage**—The year grapes are harvested; a reflection of the weather's influences on a wine's style.

# Resources

*Email and website addresses are current, as of June 2005. Note that websites come and go, however, and so may not be up to date.*

## Winemaking Supplies

**Wine Aroma Wheels**
Box 72239
Davis, CA 95616 USA
www.winearomawheel.com

**Art of Brewing**
Chessington, Surrey
United Kingdom
0208.397.2111
www.art-of-brewing.co.uk

**Beer & Wine Hobby**
Woburn, Massachusetts, USA
781.933.8818
email: shop@beer-wine.com
website:  www.beer-wine.com

**The Compleat Winemaker**
Saint Helena, California, USA
707.963.9681
www.tcw-web.com

**Crosby and Baker Ltd.**
Several locations in USA
800.999.2440
email: info@crosby-baker.com
website: www.crosby-baker.com
*Wholesaler, but a good source of information*

**E.C. Kraus**
Independence, Missouri, USA
816.254.7448
email: customerservice@eckraus.com
website: www.ECKraus.com

**Funk Winemaking Supplies**
Jordan Station, Ontario, Canada
LOR 1S0
905.562.5900
www.vaxxine.com/fwine

**Home Beer, Wine, and Cheesemaking Shop**
Woodland Hills, California, USA
818.884.8586
800.559.9922 in California
www.homebeerwinecheese.com

**G.W. Kent, Inc.**
Ann Arbor, Michigan, USA
800.333.4288
www.gwkent.com

**Midwest Homebrewing and Winemaking Supplies**
Minneapolis, Minnesota, USA
888.449.2739
www.midwestsupplies.com

**Napa Fermentation Supplies**
Napa, California, USA
707.255.6372
www.napafermentation.com

**Presque Isle Wine Cellars**
North East, Pennsylvania, USA
800.488.7492
www.piwine.com

**St. Patrick's of Texas**
Austin, Texas, USA
512.989.9727
www.StPats.com

## Vineyard Supplies

**The Growers Supply Center**
Maryland, USA
410.931.3111

**Innovative Fence Systems**
New York, USA
315.597.1111

**Jim's Supply Co., Inc.**
Several locations in California, USA
800.423.8016
www.jimssupply.com

**Orchard Valley Supply**
Harrisburg, North Carolina, USA
888.755.0098
www.orchardvalleysupply.com

**Spec Trellising**
Pennsylvania, USA
800.237.4594
www.spectrellising.com

## Education

*Many of the following are good sources of information on wine-making, grapegrowing, and wine appreciation. Some may offer classes in viticulture and/or enology.*

**American Institute of Wine and Food**
Napa, California, USA
800.274.2493
www.aiwf.org

**American Wine Society**
Durham, North Carolina, USA
919.403.0022
email:
dautlick@americanwinesociety.org
website:
www.americanwinesociety.com

**Cellarnotes.net**
www.cellarnotes.net

**Cornell University**
Ithaca, New York, USA
www.nysaes.cornell.edu

**Lallemand Company**
www.lallemandwine.us
*Manufacturers of yeast products,
including Lalvin and Bacchus wine
yeasts. Wholesale only, but website
offers valuable information on winemaking, yeast FAQs, and grape
varieties.*

**Plumpton College**
East Sussex, United Kingdom
0127.3890.454
email: enquiries@plumpton.ac.uk
website: www.plumpton.ac.uk

**St. George and Sutherland
Community College**
Jannali, New South Wales, Australia
61.02.9528.3344
email: enquiries@sgscc.nsw.edu.au
website: www.sgscc.nsw.edu.au

**Tasters Guild International**
954.928.2823
email: jjschagrin@aol.com
website: www.tastersguild.com

**University of Adelaide**
Adelaide, South Australia
61.8.8303.4455
www.adelaide.edu.au

**University of California at Davis
Viticulture & Enology**
Davis, California, USA
530.752.0380
wineserver.ucdavis.edu

**Wine Access Magazine**
Calgary, Alberta, Canada
403.240.9055 ext. 262
email: msong@redpointmedia.ca
website: www.wineaccess.ca

**Wine Education Service**
Greenford, Middlesex, England
United Kingdom
0208.991.8212/3
email:
info@wine-education-service.co.uk
website:
www.wine-education-service.co.uk

**The Wine Institute**
San Francisco, California, USA
415.512.1051
www.wineinstitute.com
*Designed largely for commercial
growers in California, but the site
does have useful links and information on wine laws, research, and
education.*

**Wyeast Laboratories Inc.**
Odell, Oregon, USA
541.354.1335
www.wyeastlab.com
*Wholesale to wineries and wine
shops only, but a good source of
information about yeasts.*

## Online Retail Wine Shops

*Note that wine shops are prohibited
by law to ship wines to certain
states. Check the website's shipping
policy before ordering wines.
However, even if you cannot order
wine from a particular online wine
shop, these sites are good sources of
information on wines that you may
be able to find locally. They can also
be good sources of wine accessories,
such as wine glasses and other gift
items for wine connoisseurs.*

**67 Wine**
USA
www.67wine.com

**The Australian Wine Center**
Australia
www.auswine.com.au

**Brown Derby International
Wine Center**
USA
www.brownderby.com

**John Armit Wines Ltd.**
United Kingdom
www.armit.co.uk

**John Hart Fine Wine**
USA
312.482.9996
www.johnhartfinewine.com

**L'Assemblage Ltd.**
United Kingdom
http://domain664185.sites.fasthosts
.com/

**MacArthur Beverages**
USA
www.bassins.com

**Marquis Wine Cellars**
Canada
www.marquis-wines.com

**Premier Cru**
USA
www.premiercru.net

**Rare Wine Co.**
USA
www.rarewineco.com

**Sherry Lehmann Wines & Spirits**
USA
www.sherry-lehmann.com

**D. Sokolin Co.**
USA
www.sokolin.com

**The Wine Cellar**
Canada
780.488.WINE
www.thewinecellar.ab.ca

**wine.com**
USA
www.wine.com

**Wine House**
Australia
www,winehouse.com.au

## Grapevine Nurseries
**Double A Vineyards**
Fredonia, New York, USA
716.672.8493
www.doubleavineyards.com

**Foster Grapevines**
North Collins, New York, USA
800.223.2211

**Grafted Grapevine Nursery**
Clifton Springs, New York, USA
315.462.3288
www.graftedgrapevines.com

**Lincoln Peak Nursery**
New Haven, Vermont, USA
802.388.7368
www.lincolnpeakvineyard.com

**Mori Vines Inc.**
Oliver, British Columbia, Canada
250.498.3350
email: info@morivines.com
website: www.morivines.com

**Novavine Grapevine Nursery**
Santa Rosa, California, USA
707.539.5678
www.novavine.com

**Sunraysia Nurseries**
Gol Gol, New South Wales,
Australia
03.5024.8502
www.sunraysianurseries.com.au

**Sunridge Nurseries**
Bakersfield, California, USA
661.363.8463
www.sunridgenurseries.com

**The Vine House**
Huddersfield, England
United Kingdom
014.848.65964
email:
sales@thevinehouse.fsnet.co.uk
website: www.thevinehouse.co.uk

## Grape and Juice Suppliers
*Many also sell equipment.*

**American Wine Grape Distributors**
Everett, Massachusetts, USA
617.387.6107
www.americanwinegrape.com

**California Wine Grape Co.**
California, USA
313.841.0590

**Kamil Juices**
Guelph, Ontario, Canada
519.824.1624
www.kamiljuices.com

**M & M Produce**
Hartford, Connecticut, USA
888.378.4884
email: sales@juicegrape.com
website: www.juicegrape.com

**The Valley Vintner**
Dublin, California, USA
866.812.9463
email: sales@valleyvintner.com
website: www.valleyvintner.com

**Walkers Fruit Basket and
Press House**
New York, USA
716.679.1292

## Publications

### Magazines
*The Australian and New Zealand
Wine Industry Journal*
Winetitles Pty Ltd.
Adelaide, South Australia
www.winetitles.com.au

*Decanter*
IPC Media, London, England
United Kingdom
www.decanter.com

*Practical Winery and Vineyard*
PWV Incorporated
Callifornia, USA
www.practicalwinery.com

*Vineyard & Winery Management*
Vineyard and Winery Services, Inc.
New York, USA
www.vwm-online.com

*Wine East*
Lancaster, Pennsylvania, USA
www.wineeast.com

*Wine Enthusiast Magazine*
Wine Enthusiast Companies
Elmsford, New York, USA
www.winemag.com

*WineMaker*
Battenkill Communications
Vermont, USA
www.winemakermag.com

*Wine Spectator*
M. Shanken Communications
New York, USA
www.winespectator.com

## Books

*Basic Guide to Pruning*
*American Wine Society Manual #1*
J.R. McGrew, American Wine
Society, 1983
*Good explanations of the basics of*
*pruning*

*From Vines to Wines*
Jeff Cox, Storey Publishing, 1999
*A nuts-and-bolts book geared to the*
*home grapegrower and winemaker*

*Grapes into Wine*
Philip Wagner,
Alfred A. Knopf, 1976
*Very well written, for both the home*
*and commercial winemaker*

*Guide to Wine Grapes*
Jancis Robinson,
Oxford University Press, 1996
*A small reference book on the*
*origins and characteristics of more*
*than 800 winegrape varieties*

*Knowing and Making Wine*
Emile Peynaud,
John Wiley and Sons, 1984
*The best professional book on wine-*
*making*

*Modern Winemaking*
Philip Jackisch,
Cornell University Press, 1985
*A very scientific approach to home*
*winemaking*

*The New France*
Andrew Jefford,
Mitchell Beazley, 2002
*An excellent survey of the new*
*progressive winemakers of France*

*Soil, Irrigation and Nutrition*
Phil Nicholas, South Australia
Research and Development
Institute, 2004
*Fairly technical Australian publica-*
*tion; good soils and nutritional infor-*
*mation*

*Sunlight into Wine*
Richard Smart and Mike Robinson,
Winetitles, 1991
*The canopy management bible; a*
*must-have guide for the quality-*
*oriented grapegrower*

*The Taste of Wine*
Emile Peynaud,
The Wine Appreciation Guild, 1983
*Fairly technical, more for professio-*
*nals, on how to critically taste wine*

*Vineyard Simple*
Tom Powers,
Alhambra Valley Publications, 2002
*Basic, how-to guide in getting a*
*small vineyard started*

*Vines, Grapes and Wines*
Jancis Robinson,
Mitchell Beazley, 1986
*An in-depth look at the major grape*
*varieties of the world*

*Winegrape Berry Sensory*
*Assessment in Australia*
Erika Winter, John Whiting and
Jacques Rousseau, Winetitles, 2004
*Excellent information and photos on*
*determining when to pick for wine*
*style*

*A Wine-Grower's Guide*
Philip Wagner, Wine Appreciation
Guild, 1996
*A good first book for the home*
*grapegrower*

## Sources for Wine Books

Amazon
www.amazon.com

Barnes & Noble
www.barnes&noble.com

The Wine Appreciation Guild Ltd.
www.wineappreciation.com
*Large collection of wine books,*
*education, and accessory materials*

Winetitles
www.winetitles.com.au

Practical Winery and Vineyards
Bookshelf
415.479.5819
www.practicalwinery.com

# Index

# Photographer Credits

**All photography by Fred Stocker with the exception of the following:**

© Cephas Picture Library/Alamy, 60-61; 82

Cornell University, NYSAES, 62; 63; 64; 65

© Cosmo Condina/Alamy, 122-123

Guillaume DeLaubier, 73; 132; 148

Jon Gnass/Gnass Photo Images, 2; 9; 18; 23; 28; 41

© Marc Grimberg/Alamy, 100-101

Mick Hales, 56

Douglas Keister/www.keisterphoto.com, 10 (bottom)

Wernher Krutein/www.photovault.com, 92; 159

Courtesy of Lallemand, 6 (bottom); 20 (bottom); 77 (bottom); 94 (top);
   95; 96; 97; 98; 104; 108; 118; 146; 149; 164; 165

Jim Law, 43; 106; 116; 117

Courtesy of Lesaffre Yeast Corporation, 94 (bottom)

Maslowski Productions, 67

Clive Nichols/www.clivenichols.com, 11 (top)

Allan Penn, 7 (top); 138 (top); 142

Clive and Sue Taylor, 68; 70; 72; 76; 77 (top); 138 (bottom); 141

Courtesy of Robert Zerkowitz, Wine Institute/www.wineinstitute.org,
   5; 126

Scot Zimmerman, 10 (top); 152-153

**Illustrations by Michael Yatcko**

# Acknowledgments

Thanks go to:

My mother, Nancy Law, who taught me by example how to be comfortable in the kitchen and how to trust my palate.

My father, Richard Law, who shared his new-found enthusiasm for tasting, enjoying, and learning about wine in moderation with his teenage son.

My editor/co-writer, Pat Price, who has a gift for motivating others. Although not a winemaker, Pat fully grasps the concept of *élevage*: when to encourage, when to push, when to intervene, when to have the courage to do nothing.

# About the Author

Jim Law fell in love with farming as an agricultural Peace Corps Volunteer in the Congo in the 1970s. On his return stateside, he combined his love of wine and farming, worked as a "cellar rat" in Ohio, and then took a wine-making job in Virginia in 1981. Jim is now the owner/winegrower of Linden Vineyards, a small winery on the Virginia Blue Ridge, an hour from Washington, DC. When not in his vineyard or cellar, he enjoys teaching, writing for trade journals, cooking, and of course, tasting wine.